Value Creation in Management Accounting

Value Creation in Management Accounting

Using Information to Capture Customer Value

CJ McNair-Connolly, Lidija Polutnik,
Riccardo Silvi, and Ted Watts

business**expert**
Press

First published in 2013 by
Business Expert Press, LLC
222 East 46th Street, New York, NY 10017
www.businessexpertpress.com

ISBN-13: 978-1-60649-620-6 (paperback)
ISBN-13: 978-1-60649-621-3 (e-book)

Business Expert Press Managerial Accounting collection

Collection ISSN: 2152-7113 (print)
Collection ISSN: 2152-7121 (electronic)

Cover and interior design by Exeter Premedia Services Private Ltd., Chennai, India

First edition: 2013

10 9 8 7 6 5 4 3 2 1

Printed in the United States of America.

Abstract

Value creation is at the heart of an economic enterprise, defining its capability to serve customers and generate profits and growth. This fact has led to an ever-increasing set of tools and techniques that start with customers, focusing on serving their preferences from the very inception of a product until its disposal. To date, most of these techniques have been only partially adopted in management accounting. This is unfortunate, because much of the data required to adequately implement a value creation approach has its roots in the Management Accounting System (MAS). The resulting model is called the Value-based Cost Management System (VCMS).

This book is principally designed for managers who want to take the lessons learned in product development, process management, and marketing and extend it to their MAS. It seeks to make this transformation of the MAS both logical and easy to implement, with a focus on the new types of information that can be garnered when the MAS is modified to fit the value creation approach. After reading this book, a manager or executive will be equipped with the tools and techniques to both implement and use the VCMS. The resulting information will allow the company to align its efforts by creating a common language which uses the transformed accounting language to compare, evaluate, and choose the best strategic and tactical options available. After making these choices, the VCMS also allows managers to subsequently track how closely actual results come to the projected outcomes.

The results and recommendations in this book are based on action field research, where the authors have personally supported the analysis and subsequent use of the data generated. The authors of the book will provide, upon request, a simplified automated data collection template that will ease the implementation process. In total, then, this book provides a unique perspective on the organization and creates an actionable common language that allows the unification of the continuous improvement efforts of managers across an organization.

Keywords

value creation, continuous improvement, value engineering, value-added, business value-added, waste, customer value profile, value proposition, activity-based management, lean management, process management, value multipliers, incremental analysis, strategic analysis, value-based cost management system.

Contents

About the Authors

Dr. CJ McNair-Connolly is an internationally recognized expert in cost management. She has authored nine trade books on various aspects of the relationship and development of cost management and the new technologies that define modern management practice. She has also authored numerous articles in the academic and practitioner press and has given seminars and speeches on modern management practice in multiple settings and countries. Holding a MBA and PhD from Columbia University, Dr. McNair-Connolly has spent her entire career conducting field research studies, using this knowledge to create new theory in management accounting and control systems. These studies have been done as pure academic exercises and as a form of action research. In doing this work, she has accumulated extensive field experience and knowledge that shapes her writing and theory development. Dr. McNair-Connolly currently is an Honorary Principal Fellow at the University of Wollongong. She can be contacted at cjconnolly126@gmail.com.

Dr. Lidija Polutnik is a professor and Chair of the Economics Division at Babson College in Boston, MA. Dr. Polutnik has done research and consulted in the area of pricing, revenue management, and strategic cost management. Her research in this area is based on the analysis of the relationship between the firm's costs and customers' value and the influence of this relationship on the firm's profit. Dr. Polutnik also conducts research in public finance and is focused on the role institutions play in market economies and specifically in countries in transition. Dr. Polutnik's work has been published in numerous academic journals and books including *The European Accounting Review*, *Advances in Management Accounting*, *Journal of Cost Management*, *Journal of Corporate Accounting and Finance*, *Industrial Relations Journal*, and *Comparative Economic Studies Journal*. Dr. Polutnik has extensive consulting and executive teaching experience in the United States and in multinational companies in the area of tactical and strategic pricing, customer value analysis, and value creation model.

She regularly teaches at the Executive MBA of Alma Graduate School at the University of Bologna, Italy. She can be contacted at polutnik@babson.edu.

Dr. Riccardo Silvi is an associate professor of Management Accounting at the School of Economics, Management and Statistics of the University of Bologna (Italy) and member of the Department of Management of the same university. He is Program Director of the Master in Accounting, Finance and Control and of the Executive MBA at the Alma Graduate School of the University of Bologna. In these programs he teaches strategic financial analysis, management accounting, performance management systems, and strategic cost management.

His research interests focus on management accounting (design of management control systems, performance measurement systems, strategic accounting), analytical business performance management, cost accounting, strategic cost management. Riccardo is affiliated researcher at Center for Performance Research & Analytics (CEPRA) at the University of Augsburg, Germany, and was visiting professor at the Faculty of Economic Sciences of the Georg-August, Göttingen University. He was visiting professor at Babson College (Boston), at the University of Sydney and at the McQuarie Graduate School of Management of Sydney. Riccardo's work has been published in numerous academic journals and books including the *The European Accounting Review, Advances in Management Accounting, Journal of Operation Management, Cost Management, Journal of Intellectual Capital, International, and Journal of Productivity and Performance Management.* He has assisted many leading Italian companies in strategic cost and value management programs. He can be contacted at riccardo.silvi@unibo.it.

Dr. Ted Watts is an assistant professor in the School of Accounting & Finance at the University of Wollongong, Australia. He has held positions of Associate Head of School and Head of Discipline and has served on the University Academic Senate and the University Education Committee. His teaching experience includes The University of New South Wales, The University of Technology, Sydney, and teaching assignments in Shanghai, Hong Kong, Malaysia, and the United States of America.

Ted has published widely, including articles in *Critical Perspectives on Accounting, Financial Accountability and Management, Journal of Accounting & Organizational Change, Journal of Cost Management, Journal of Corporate Accounting & Finance, JASSA: The Finica Journal of Applied Finance, Australasian Journal of Regional Studies, Australasian Accounting, Business and Finance Journal, International Journal of Critical Accounting, Accounting Forum, Advances in Public Interest Accounting* and the *Journal of Applied Accounting Research.*

His research interests include strategic cost management, capacity management, and value creation. These interests together with his research output and several reach awards have secured him research grants with CPA Australia, the Accounting and Finance Association of Australia and New Zealand and the Association of Superannuation Funds of Australia. He can be contacted at tedw@uow.edu.au.

CHAPTER 1

A Focus on the Customer

The value of all things, even our lives, depends on the use we make of them.[1]

Value creation is at the heart of an economic enterprise, defining its capability to serve customers and generate profits and growth. This fact has led to an ever-increasing set of tools and techniques that start with customers, focusing on serving their preferences from the very inception of a product until its disposal. Most of these tools and techniques are based in either marketing or product development, with a constant eye toward helping companies capture more of the value created with their industry chains.

The focus of this book is on one specific, and overlooked, perspective on value creation—management accounting. Using the results of many years of field data collection, analysis, and development, a comprehensive model that captures the essence of the value creation process in diverse organizations is presented. Two key perspectives are taken into consideration in the discussion. First, the book emphasizes how companies can increase the value they create for customers—enhancing their product/service value proposition—by effective design of their products and services. This value needs to be effectively communicated to customers so that they can incorporate it in their buying decision.

The second major perspective is internally focused—helping companies eliminate the nonvalue-added activities that build waste, not value, into their products and services. By removing and minimizing wasteful work, more funds can be reinvested in value-added activities that help grow the top line of the business. It is a win-win solution that starts with understanding how customers perceive value.

The Concept of Value

Value is defined as the sum of perceived benefits received by the customer in return for the sacrifices made in terms of price paid, costs incurred, and effort spent in order to acquire a product or service.[2] Value is the result of the amount of resources (time, money, and energy) expended by the final consumer in the entire value chain. Value is not created in the interchange of goods and services between trading partners—it does not exist until a willing consumer validates its existence.[3] All trading partners contribute to the final value of a product or service as defined by the consumer, but they do not create value until the final consumer makes the decision to purchase the good or service at a specified price.

These facts place the consumer, as final arbitrator of exchange value, at the center of every business organization. If there is a chain of customers (a supply chain), then companies may have to deal with conflicting demands on their time and resources. How to choose among the demands of trading partners versus those of the final consumer is straightforward— the final consumer wins the debate. Throughout this book the final consumer will be the focus, with the term "customer" meaning the final consumer, not a supply chain partner.

That being said, cost can be incurred by companies in a supply chain that no consumer will pay for. So, it simply makes good business sense to seek to optimize the product and service offerings of the firm from the customer's perspective regardless of where the company exists in the overall supply chain. Well-run companies can reap the larger shares of the consumer-defined value creation, or revenues, by managing their trading relationships efficiently and effectively. This is called value capture.[4]

Value from a Customer's Perspective

Customers have well-defined expectations regarding the benefits they want, and perceive exist, in a product or service. For instance, customers value responsiveness to their questions and concerns when dealing with a product or service provider. Responsiveness is a common *value attribute* that makes up a customer's profile, or list of valued product/service features. The customer has an entire list, consisting of multiple attributes that provide the basis for their final assessment of value delivered by a specific product or service. This list of value attributes, and the relative importance of each attribute in the buying decision, creates the opportunities for companies to maximize their reach to the consumer marketplace—to optimize their profit.

Every product or service presents the customer with a range of features, which is called the product's or service's value *proposition*. The value proposition is the sum of all the benefits promised to the customer and is the basis for customers making choices among competing products. The value proposition consists, then, of all of the value attributes embedded in a product or service. When asked to name these attributes, customers have very little trouble. Customers know what they are buying and why. While their reasons can range from something as specific as the size or weight of a product, through functionality, and even on to statements such as the product "makes me look cool," customers can detail their wants (their *value profile*) and assess how closely a specific product or service matches their needs and wants.

Figure 1.1 summarizes the value creation process from a customer's perspective. The expected benefits of the product or service are its value proposition. As noted, the expected benefits gained from these product, service, and cultural attributes depend on how closely they match the customer's own value profile—their specific wants and needs. To gain

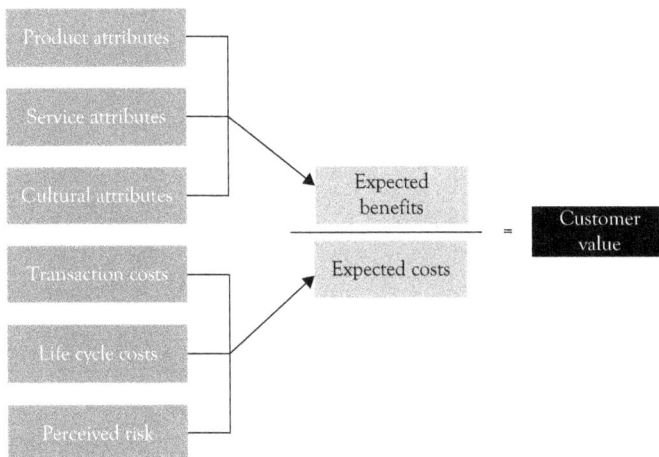

Figure 1.1. Value creation: the customer's perspective.

these benefits, a customer incurs several types of costs. These not only include the transaction cost, or price paid to acquire the product or gain access to the service—the expected costs include the product's or service's life cycle costs (total cost of ownership for its useful life) and the riskiness of the purchase decision.

The more a customer knows about a product or service, in other words the more often they purchase it, the lower the risk and overall transaction costs of the purchase. For instance, the decision to buy paper towels is shaped by the cumulative experience the customer has had with the specific brand of paper towels. Risk is low and the need to do prepurchase research is also low (low transaction costs), so the decision is easy to make.

When we talk about a major purchase, though, such as the purchase of a kitchen stove, a new car, or a new home, the decision becomes much more complex for the customer. Risk may be high because the decision comes with a high price tag and uncertainty regarding actual functionality and life cycle costs. The customer doesn't make this decision often, so the search for information prior to purchase ramps up the transaction costs and risk even more. Clearly not all customers are equally informed, but all are faced with a much riskier choice when large ticket items are purchased than when daily usage items are obtained.

Let's think about a fairly large purchase decision for a customer— choosing the windows for a new or existing home. While there are a broad range of providers of windows, the consumer has narrowed the choice down to two of the top selling brands—Andersen Windows and Pella Windows. The value attributes and relative weightings for the two different companies' windows are in Figure 1.2.

Value attribute	Andersen Windows	Pella Windows
Quality	High	Moderately high
Durability	High	Moderate
Sizes available	Moderate	High
Appearance	High	High
Shapes available	Low	High
Reputation of firm	High	Moderately high

Figure 1.2. Comparative value propositions.

The value attributes driving the decision are the quality of the product, its durability, size selection, overall appearance, shapes available (design), and reputation of the firm. For a customer whose primary focus is on quality, durability, and reputation of the firm, Andersen Windows is the obvious choice. If, on the other hand, the customer is more concerned with choice in sizes and design to add an architectural feel to their home, they would tend to buy from Pella. Since an entire group of windows is purchased at once, the style variables can become quite important to the competiveness of the firm. They also lead to two different companies with two different value propositions for a window. The result is two very different customer value *segments*.

A Market-based View of a Company's Value Creation Profile

Armed with this basic terminology, we can now create a different perspective on the challenge faced by a company in the marketplace. This perspective is provided in Figure 1.3. While the customer's final choice

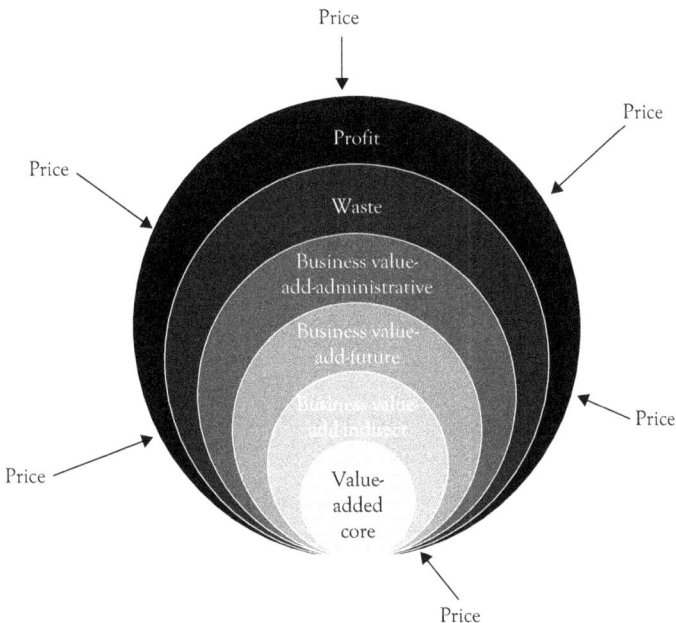

Figure 1.3. Value creation: a market perspective.

of one product over another is based on the total package of value attributes provided, the choice decision translates this process into a single dimension—the price the selling company receives for the product or service provided.

We now see several things of interest. First, the value-added core of attributes that customers have used in their purchase decision now makes up only part of the cost the company incurs in providing the product or service. For a well-run company, it is normal for this value-added core of attributes to consume 20–25% of the total costs of the firm. Clearly, there are other things the company spends its scarce resources on. To denote the majority of these, we've coined the term business value-add to recognize that there is a *reason* for the activities, just not one the customer directly values.

The first layer is denoted as "business value-add—indirect." These are many of the support services that are critical to long-term relationships with a customer but that the customer is not willing to pay for directly. For instance, a company has to issue an invoice when it sells a good or service. The customer doesn't want to pay the company for the activity of issuing an invoice, but the customer can become very dissatisfied if the invoice is wrong, requiring more investment of their time and effort to correct. The fact that these activities impact overall customer satisfaction with their relationship with a firm have led many researchers to place them in a category called "service logic" and to make them part of the value-added core.[5] This amount has been included in value-add by some companies we've done research with and excluded by others. The term "indirect" is used simply because the customer tends not to pay attention to these activities unless there is an error—they serve as potential dissatisfiers, not value creators.

The next layer is business value-add—future. Included here are all of the R&D, strategic, and marketing activities of the firm. For investors, these are very important activities, but for the current customer they are not. Why? Because the customer has already made a purchase decision based on existing offerings. It is doubtful if they want to pay the company to have their purchase decision made outdated. New customers are influenced by these new options, which are the life blood of the long-term health of the firm, but they are not of value to today's customers and hence don't garner any price.

Attention is next focused on all of the business value-add—administrative activities of the company. Some researchers call these nonvalue-add activities, but it is very difficult to actually implement a system where some peoples' entire job gets called nonvalue-added. And, in reality, the company cannot exist if someone doesn't tend to payroll, for instance. These activities are more (or less) required for the business to operate. They are activities, though, which sometimes can be eliminated or reduced by using different procedures or technologies. At the end they should be limited to only the essentials because they will never earn a dollar of revenue for the firm—they are pure cost with no redeeming features for the customer. As we'll see shortly, we want to capture this information in our management accounting model so we can monitor and control where each valuable dollar earned as revenue is spent.

The next circle in the diagram is termed "waste." These activities are often the focus of lean Six Sigma efforts, where attention is paid to eliminating unnecessary work wherever it occurs. This is such an important topic that an entire chapter will be devoted to it. For now, waste should simply be thought of as all of the "re's" and "un's" (undo, for instance) that customers will not pay for and that will never provide a benefit to anyone involved in the organization. Waste exists everywhere, in every activity, and in every organization. It is the potential gold that can be mined to improve profitability.

The final circle is the profit ring. If the company produces a product or service that is valued by the market, and they haven't spent too much doing the required work or wasted too much, then there should be some profit left in the transaction with the customer. Note, though, that profit is not guaranteed by the market. Price is set based on attributes and how well they match customers' desires. It is an ever-shrinking amount. Cost and waste occur. The company must manage its internal activities well in order to actually profit from the price customers are willing to pay for all of the activities a company undertakes in serving them.

Using Value to Create a New Accounting

We have now charted out the economics of the firm in a way that allows us to match our accounting to the realities faced by the firm. Let's start with the revenue received for a specific product or service. We know this revenue is earned based on the value attributes, and we can use customers' data to define how important each attribute was to the purchase decision. Armed with this information, we can now break the revenue line down into a set of revenue equivalents, or the amount of the total revenue that is earned by each value *attribute*. Why do we want this information? We want it because it helps us focus internal attention on those things customers care about. This approach to the accounting model also brings the financial team into sync with the marketing and strategy teams. It creates a common language that shifts the concept of revenue from a one-dimensional outcome to a multidimensional management tool.

In such a value-based cost management system (VCMS), the goal is always to match revenue with its costs. Here is where we begin to flesh out the accounting model to use a market perspective. Using activity-based analysis tools, individuals or managers in the firm are asked to list the activities performed in their area and assign approximate weights to the amount of time (and hence expense) each activity represents in their area. Having defined an activity and its related cost, attention now turns to adding "tags" to the data element to match the market perspective. Specifically, each activity is analyzed to determine what percentage of value-add, business value-add, and waste it has. Note that each activity is analyzed across all five possible dimensions of costs. This is a significant improvement over the existing literature that tends to place an entire activity into either value-added or nonvalue-added categories.

The VCMS model is not complete yet, though. We need to tie these activities to the revenue line using the value attributes. For every activity, then, that has some portion of judged customer value-add in it, the manager or individual assigns that value-added portion across the various attributes, completing the linkage of the accounting model to the marketing model that dominates the rest of the firm. Done with spreadsheet support, this is an exercise that yields tremendous insights into the firm.

Using these techniques, revenue has now been matched to its value-added costs. In addition, knowledge has been gained about the amount of business value-add and waste currently taking place. If a decision has been made to add indirect business value-add costs to the value-added costs, it is a simple mathematical task to revise the numbers.

More has been gained than a simple snapshot of where the money comes in and where it goes, though. Because revenue and costs have both been defined around value attributes, a company can now assess whether it is spending its money in areas that are best suited to customer requirements. This is accomplished by dividing the revenue by attribute by the value-added costs by attribute to get a revenue *multiplier*. If the multiplier is very low (less than five), it means the company is spending too much money on that attribute. Why five? Since value-added costs have been found across the board, in industry after industry and company after company to be about 20% of total costs, there is an inherent revenue multiplier of five in every profitable organization.

The real challenge comes when the multiplier is very high (eight or above). Here the question becomes two-sided—is this an area where the company has a competitive advantage because they create so much value with minimal cost or is it an area where the firm is underspending, failing to deliver desired value to its customers? To answer this question, customer satisfaction data becomes critical. If customers are satisfied with the firm's performance on a key attribute, then a high multiplier signals a competitive advantage. If the satisfaction level is low, though, then the firm is opening itself to lost sales and competitive failure.

This brief overview of the accounting model, which we call a value-based cost management system, is built around value creation. The goal is simply to provide enough working knowledge to understand how each of the subsequent in-depth chapters fits into the overall architecture. Figure 1.4 reviews the steps that are taken in creating a VCMS.

Completing these seven steps can be done very efficiently and effectively using Excel-based data gathering tools. As we'll see, we can even add another step, namely placing a process code on each activity to support the integration of the data away from a departmental structure to a process structure. The objective of this book is not only to go into further detail on the basic features of the VCMS, but also to provide a basic implementation plan that includes specific information on how to structure the data collection process to optimize the information it creates for the lowest cost possible.

Step	Reason
1. Gather customer attribute data including relative weights of each attribute.	This serves as the basis for the entire model.
2. Derive revenue equivalents.	These numbers provide us with the key information of how much revenue is earned on each attribute.
3. Gather activity data across all departments.	This information provides an understanding of resource consumption.
4. Subcategorize activity data into value-add, business value-add, and waste.	These data provide the means to compare spending to value creation.
5. Categorize all value added costs by value attribute.	This allows us to create revenue multipliers.
6. Create revenue multipliers.	This information is the goal of the entire process.
7. Analyze revenue multipliers to find opportunities for improvement.	Here is where new information is gathered to help a company grow its revenue line through careful spending adjustments.

Figure 1.4. Steps to create a value-based cost management system (VCMS).

Using Value-Based Cost Management

One of the remaining questions is a simple "why?" Why should a firm invest any of its scarce resources in generating a new form of accounting information? The answer to this question lies at the very core of accounting in an organization—it is deemed to be the language of business. If it is to serve as a common language, shouldn't the accounting system use the same set of assumptions the rest of the organization uses? If a company is truly to be customer-centered, it has to collect its information in ways that shed light on whether they are making the best choices to capture customer value. Looking out, not in, has to become the key feature of accounting in a customer-driven organization.

In the companies that have used this approach, new strategic insights have been gained. The benefits of a common language have allowed the information to be accepted and used in everything from operational to strategic decisions and from product and service delivery to the very design of these offerings. With the addition of process coding, companies have been able to unite all of their new management techniques under one umbrella of accounting logic and calculation. Moreover, tracking value multipliers over time allows a company to monitor value creation dynamics, and assess its market opportunities and threats. It is a system that is easy to understand, easy to use, and critical for the long-term health of an organization.

Clearly, a system such as this doesn't replace the financial accounting model. That exists to support the questions asked by company shareholders and to fulfill other obligations of companies. The goal is not to provide information to external parties but rather to support the initiatives taken by internal managers to better serve their company's customers—to use accounting information to grow the top line.

Managing customers as assets requires measuring, managing, and maximizing them.[6]

CHAPTER 2

Customer Value-Add and Its Impact on Revenue

…value is the primary influence on purchase decisions and the leading indicator of revenue growth, profitability, and competitive advantage.[1]

Customer value-add is the complete set of features and benefits provided by a good or service. What makes any feature or benefit value-added is the fact that a consumer is making a choice to sacrifice time and money and take on inherent risk to obtain the good or service. As we have seen in the previous chapter, though, when we take the concept of value-add inside the organization, we have to recognize that value is created through a series of activities. In addition, even inherently value-creating activities can contain some levels of business value-add and waste. Separating the value-adding aspects of business activities from their counterparts is the objective of value-based cost management systems (VCMS).

The literature on value creation has two primary foci: customers and shareholders. While it is clear that organizations create value for their shareholders when they make a profit, it is obvious that no shareholder value can be created unless some consumer need is met. *Value capture* references the ability of a firm to seize the largest share of the total value created for the consumer within the industry value chain. Throughout this book, the emphasis is on the consumer. Customers are defined as being end users who actually establish the monetary value of the products and services offered by firms in a value chain. Having clarified the focus of the discussion, let's now turn to the concept of value attributes.

Defining Value Attributes

The key challenge for a successful business is to understand customer needs. In the current global and intensely competitive environment, it is more important than ever to both understand, and leverage, the relationship between customer requirements (value) and the costs and competencies required to meet these expectations.

A customer-focused organization understands the central role played by its value proposition in defining the firm's overall revenue potential. A product's economic value can be defined as the price of the customer's best alternative (reference value) plus the value of attributes that differentiate the product from its alternatives.[2] To understand value from the customer's perspective is to gain the power to grow the top line of the business, a firm's revenues which are essential to sustainable growth. While marketing and sales functions have used customer value information to target and effectively position a firm's products and services within specific customer segments, this knowledge is not as consistently used to discipline the firm's spending on resources and activities—its *cost structure*. The result is the *cost–value gap*, a schism between the market and the firm that if left in place can destroy both a company's profits and its future.

The cost–value gap is the difference between customer preferences for specific product or service features, called attributes, and the cost of the product being offered by the firm. A simple illustration of this gap as identified at a large electronics firm is presented in Figure 2.1.[3] On the left side of the illustration is a list of the five primary activities completed by the firm's customer service group, along with the percentages of the total customer service budget spent on each activity. As can be seen, producing and revising manuals consumes 70% of the total customer service budget, with direct contact customer service activities comprising the other 30% of the budget.

Looking at the firm from the customer's perspective, a very different picture of the importance of the firm's service activities emerges. Specifically, manual availability and updates represent only 10% of the total service value proposition. Direct contact customer service activities are what the customer values, as evidenced by the 90% combined

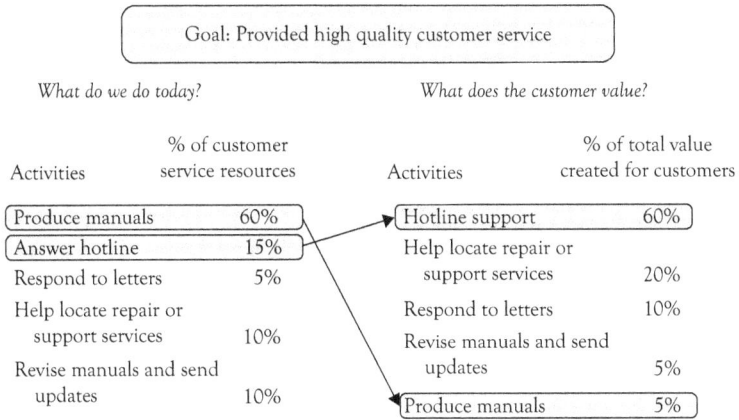

Figure 2.1. The cost–value gap.

weighting of these activities by the firm's customers. In the customers' eyes, 89% of what the firm spends on manuals is waste.[4] The company has failed to align its resources and activities with customer value preferences, and thereby reduced its potential amount of profit.

Activities in the right column of Figure 2.1 could be defined as overall service responsiveness. What the list of activities shows us is that we need the detail we get from an activity analysis, combined with the logic of the VCMS, to really operationalize this attribute in a way that allows the company to improve its service responsiveness. Companies cannot identify which activities are value-adding without understanding the relative importance of specific features/attributes valued by the customer. Bringing the customer's perspective into the equation is always the essence of managing a customer-driven organization.

What this example illustrates is the fact that value attributes are themselves composed of a variety of value activities that the firm performs in order to meet customer expectations. Unless a firm has a clear understanding of what customers expect in terms of service responsiveness, they could be spending significant sums of money on performing a variety of activities without delivering what is desired by the customer. This is a lesson that has been learned in the design for manufacturability movement—that including the customer's perspective provides the firm with the necessary knowledge to define exactly what a specific attribute means in actionable terms.

To be considered a value-added activity, then, the activity has to be one that customers value and are able to evaluate in terms of its impact on their ultimate satisfaction with a product or service. Value-added is an external, customer-driven perspective.

The Value Proposition

The entire list of features and capabilities offered by a firm's product is its value proposition. This proposition is established during the design phase and can be very hard to change once the product or service is launched. Services are more responsive to the need to make downstream changes, but there is always a lag in terms of getting the focus to match customer expectations. It is expensive and time-consuming to try to correct the value proposition offered by a product/service bundle. It is critical to include the customer as soon as possible in the design phase so the resulting product actually hits its market target.

What is a value attribute, then? It is a specific feature of a product or service that the customer recognizes and places value on when making a purchase decision. Products and services create value for customers in a variety of ways: ease of use, performance, quality, service responsiveness, fashion sense, etc. It is important to understand that the customer and not the firm is the judge of whether these attributes create customer value and better satisfy his/her needs. When a bundle of value attributes is combined in a final good or service, a company establishes its value proposition.

In our field work, we have found that managers often don't have an accurate view of customer preferences or the weight of their importance in customer decisions. Becoming a customer-driven organization means the customer plays an active role in all product/service decisions. The first order of business, then, is to include the customer perspective early in the process of developing a product's or service's value proposition.

When we look at the entire value proposition of a firm, we usually end up with a list of five to eight items the customer cares about. If we add to this information how important each attribute is to the total value provided by a product or service, we can end up with a spider chart that looks something like Figure 2.2. This is the list of value attributes for a typical cell phone.

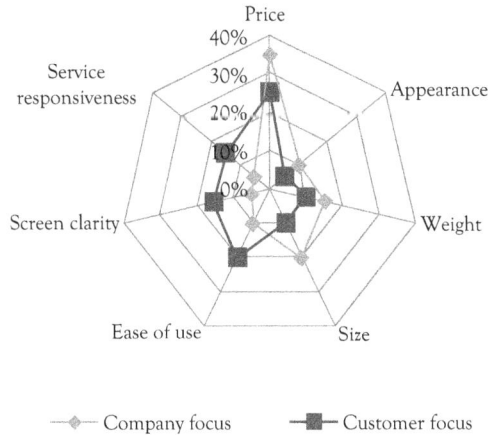

Figure 2.2. A spider's view of value.

Notice that this chart has a very specific characteristic—*all of the weights assigned to the value attributes add up to 100%.* Why is this important? It is the critical assumption required to transform the attribute data into something that can be used in the accounting framework. Accounting has to add up. Any accounting system that doesn't "balance" is unlikely to receive strong support from senior members of the management team, who remember this lesson very well from their basic accounting classes.

In developing and designing a VCMS, then, it is important to link together key marketing managers with the financial analysis people who are given responsibility for the revenue and cost aspects of the model. This is where the common language component of the VCMS originates. Different functional areas in the organization, specifically marketing and finance, have to agree on the language and focus when collecting customer information using the same metrics, ones that can bridge the gap between different areas of the firm.

Different methodologies exist for obtaining information on the valuation of customer attributes. Conjoint analysis has the objective of capturing the value of trade-offs in product features in a systematic way and to assign monetary value to specific attributes. Customers are presented with choices of similar products whose prices and features are different and are forced to choose a product they prefer. For technical and industrial products it is often possible to accurately measure the value of attributes by quantifying such features as reduced failure rates, and reduced labor costs, which then allows the firm to compute the value of the feature. Other customer value assessment tools, which are often used for value quantification, are indirect surveys, customer focus groups, and importance ratings.

Vague references to "important" versus "not important" cannot provide the specificity required to link accounting information to the marketing perspective. Having customers assign specific weights to attributes is a small adjustment to marketing analysis with major benefits for the firm. And, customers can provide this information—they inherently weight each value attribute when they are making their purchase decisions. Once monetary values are determined for the features for each identified market segment, the whole organization benefits by understanding exactly what and how much value each type of customer places on what the organization is producing. Marketing gains from this approach as it provides stronger metrics to use in the marketing models used to perform segmentation analysis. It is a change that is for the best for all involved parties, including the customers who ends up with a supplier that is much more knowledgeable about what they value and why.

Price and the Value Proposition

Customers make purchase decisions based on economic value and price paid compared with internal reference prices. The internal reference price is the price level that is expected to be "fair" for the product category.[5] Customers form internal reference prices over time and they tend to frame actual purchase decisions and actual prices relative to this reference price. Reference price represents something best thought of as "table stakes." It is the commodity nature of the product—features that all products in this market have to have to even be considered by a customer in the purchase decision.

Going back to our window example, price can be connected to the basic features of any window. It has to let in light but keep out the elements. These basic features of a window are non-negotiable. A window that doesn't let in light or that fails to keep the rain out of the house would not be considered by a customer—at least not by many. Price, then, lays down the reference/commodity baseline for a product class, including all of the things that the product or service has to be able to do.

What are the table stakes for a cell phone? It has to be able to send and receive phone calls, and in today's world, text messages and video clips. To do this effectively, a cell phone needs some basic electronics and a good antenna. If the phone can't meet the basic requirements of the consumer it won't be considered in the purchase decision. The challenge for a company is to understand exactly what features, and in what amounts, are critical for a product to be considered as a competitive offering. While this basic list will vary by customer type, it is also quite likely that customers that expect more from the product will be willing to pay a higher price for a *differentiated* offering.

In other words, price plays a key role in the strategic sense. It helps a company separate out those features that have to be in a basic offering that is positioned to compete on price alone versus a product or service that commands a premium in the market because it does something extra that the customer values. A company with an undifferentiated product will see most of the weighting in its customers' value proposition collapse into a reference price. This is a difficult competitive position to maintain, as cost cutting becomes the only way to increase profits. It's hard to grow the top line in an industry where products have become commodities.

Price, then, is defined by basic features, the baseline for a product to even enter into any customer's purchase decision. The lower price is in the total weighting of attributes, the more important it is for the firm to differentiate itself on other features of the product or service. Knowing the table stakes of the competitive game is the first step in creating superior customer value. Throughout this book, price will be used to refer to the reference price, or table stakes element of the given product or service. This usage is made because in almost all the customer data efforts undertaken by the firms studied, the customers included price in their definition of key attributes.

Tying Value Creation to Revenue

The key innovation contained in the VCMS is the tying of value creation to specific revenue streams. The model makes the simple assumption that customer value identification results in actual revenue, transforming and strengthening the linkages between products and profits in the firm. Optimizing a firm's profits begins with recognizing that a firm is not, by definition, given a "right" by the market to cover its costs. Instead, it must earn its revenues by meeting customer requirements better than the competition. If costs are kept within the boundaries of the price envelope, then there is profit. Profit is not guaranteed to any firm. This leads to several observations:

- Only by understanding and investing in building the value-added core of activities can a firm increase its "price envelope" or revenue for a product or service.
- Costs can seldom be passed directly through to customers. Those costs that do not add value come out of profit.
- If across-the-board cost reductions are undertaken, then the value-added core is reduced and the price envelope collapses inward (less value is delivered so price decreases).
- Price is a multiplicative function of the value-added activities of the firm. This means that a dollar invested in value-added activities should deliver more than a one dollar increase in revenues as long as the firm is not overspending on a specific value attribute, given market conditions. Conversely, a dollar cut out of the value-added core will result in more than one dollar of revenue lost, creating a death spiral for the firm, under existing market conditions.
- Growth can only occur if the firm leverages its competencies in the areas that the firm's customers value by reinvesting savings from cost reduction in business value-add activities and waste to activities and investments that support the value-added core.

These are the key assumptions that underlie the VCMS. Based upon this logic, the VCMS develops a strategic analysis of the preferences (value profiles) for various customers and customer segments. This information is then used to create an assessment of firm performance in general or for a specific product/service bundle. The customer is infused throughout this process, playing a central role in all decisions.

The Role of Customer Segments

Customer value analysis often leads to the identification of customer segments. For instance, Impact Communications,[6] a public relations firm, was known in the marketplace for its "cause-based" market research. Research was the dominant focus of the owner of the firm and the research value attribute placed high on the list of attributes the firm offered to its customers.

As the firm grew, it acquired a broad range of customers with different needs. The firm, though, continued to place a heavy emphasis on providing research for its clients because it perceived that this was the area where it added the most value over its competitors. Problems began to occur as the firm started to have difficulty retaining new clients. Specifically, clients that wanted the firm to do basic public relations work (smile and dial) were dissatisfied with the service provided by the firm. Since this was the largest customer segment in terms of revenue, the problem received attention.

Of the existing $25 million in revenues, the customer base could be divided into the following segments (see Figure 2.3).

As the figure suggests, not only was Impact having trouble retaining its publicity clients, it was losing money on this segment because all of the money invested to gain new clients was having to be absorbed by one, rather than multiple, engagements.

To better understand the problem, the decision was made to explore the value attributes of the different segments. The results, which are noted in Figure 2.4, were striking. There were marked differences in what the customer segments valued. Publicity clients were mainly interested in placements quantity, or namely how many places their product or name showed up in such things as press clippings. Research clients did not care

	Publicity clients	Marketing service clients	Strategy/research clients
Revenue	$15.0	$8.5	$1.5
Operating costs	15.9	5.3	0.8
Segment profit	($0.9)	$3.2	$0.7
Profit percentage	(6%)	37.6%	46.7%

Figure 2.3. Impact customer segment profitability (in millions).

Value attribute	Publicity clients	Marketing services clients	Strategy/research clients
Placements quantity	60%	30%	0%
Creative/proactive service	15%	10%	20%
Strategy/brand service	5%	20%	60%
Knowledge of business	10%	20%	5%
Reputation	5%	5%	10%
Results merchandising	5%	15%	5%
Total	100%	100%	100%

Figure 2.4. Impact customer value attributes by segment.

about placements—they were at the firm because of its research expertise. The company was providing a "one-size-fits-all" product for a differentiated market.

Impact, as one of the early clients in the series of projects underlying the development of the VCMS, went from these unique value profiles to breaking down their internal cost structure by what value attribute was served. No attempt was made to separate out value-added costs at this early stage of the research.

What was learned at Impact Communications? That a firm can be very good at its core competency and leave most of its customers dissatisfied. Since the firm did the same work for every client and considered the placements activity as being a low-skill, undesirable task, it was failing to meet the expectations of its major customer segment—publicity clients.

Finally, during the course of the discussions the concept of "results merchandising" arose, something no one had considered. This translated to how good the individual who hired the firm looked to his or her management based on the quality of Impact's final presentation. It was a value attribute Impact had not been aware of, one that drove 15% of the value for its general marketing services clients, who were mostly other small businesses that couldn't afford their own marketing team.

Because of this work, Impact reconfigured its internal work to match up what they were doing with the customer's value profile. Specifically, they asked customers to provide a value attribute weighting at the beginning of an engagement. Management reports were then created for clients that showed the spending of engagement dollars mapped against the customer's value preferences. The power of value attributes and knowing how to best serve customer segments are a vital message contained in the results at Impact Communications.

Summary

In this chapter we have examined the concepts of value-added activities and value attributes, emphasizing how important it is to drive these concepts from the outside-in. A VCMS starts and ends with customer-defined value. By a simple transformation of customer data, namely making value attribute weightings add up to 100%, the VCMS merges accounting logic with marketing and strategy approaches to create an effective communication- and action-driving tool for management.

As we have seen so far, then, there are a number of criteria that are essential for any cost management system that seeks to support improvement in the amount and quality of a firm's value-added core. Included among these are the following:

- *Externally focused*: The information required to create and support the cycle of growth in a company is not found in the general ledger. It resides in the external market, in the minds and actions of the firm's customers. An effective VCMS has to focus on external, not internal trends and information.
- *Growth-oriented*: The cycle of growth is an investment strategy that emphasizes the rewards earned by improving the firm's alignment with customer preferences.
- *Future-oriented*: Growth requires an orientation toward the future—one that places the emphasis on ensuring that the firm is constantly adjusting its activities to meet emerging customer requirements. Scorekeeping and reporting prior results are of much less use in a growth-oriented, value-optimizing firm.
- *Profit-shaping*: While all accounting is designed to capture and report profits, a VCMS is single-mindedly dedicated to supporting profitable growth through improved alignment

of a firm's activities and outcomes with customer preferences. A VCMS proactively shapes profits—it does not simply passively report them.

- *Customer-driven*: Customers, their preferences, and their satisfaction with current performance are all key constructs in a VCMS. Cost information and analysis is aligned with market-based information that highlights customer requirements.

- *Dynamic*: The demands of the customer are constantly changing, as new features, products, and needs emerge. The customer data supporting a customer-driven strategy must also be fluid, modified as conditions change.

- *Value-based*: The activities that take place in the firm have to be analyzed to separate out their value-added component from business value-add and waste. All activities have some component of business value-add and waste, even those that are mostly value creating. Gaining this detailed knowledge at the activity level helps the VCMS support all forms of process and lean management.

- *Elegant*: The methods for data collections and analysis must be elegant in a VCMS. The need to stay close to the customer, to constantly assess firm efforts against customer requirements, and to support adjustments and action to improve customer-defined strategic alignment requires an information system that can be easily updated, used, and adjusted to meet changing conditions.

These criteria suggest a very different form of cost management, one that is used to shape strategy, not evaluate the outcomes *ex post*. The result is a proactive, externally focused, customer-driven role for cost information and cost management practice.

> *All change is not growth; all movement is not forward.*
> Ellen Glasgow[7]

CHAPTER 3

Business Value-Add: Minimizing the Activities that Reduce Customer Value

You can have big plans, but it's the small choices that have the greatest power. They draw us toward the future we want to create.

Robert Cooper[1]

Organizations spend most of their scarce resources in delivering business value-add activities. In this chapter we look at the categories of business value-add in more depth as we learn how to differentiate and categorize activities that are business-, not customer-driven.

Placing Business Value-Add in Context

The reason organizations exist is because the formal combination of talents, skills, and resources into one entity provides superior capability for meeting customer expectations and delivering value to the market more efficiently. Instead of having to enter into market transactions for every activity that needs to be done, an organization brings all of the needed inputs together under one entity. What drives the creation of organizations is the desire to lower transaction costs.

Many different organizational forms arise in the economy. For instance, many firms decide to vertically integrate, buying up their trading partners in the value chain so they can gain control over product features, price, quality, and the timeliness to market. Other firms decide to go "virtual," focusing on keeping direct control of only core competencies and outsourcing all other activities to other companies in the marketplace. General Electric is an example of a firm that pursues vertical integration, while Nike is known for being one of the top virtual firms in the world.

Whether vertically integrated or virtual, all companies have to deliver the basic functions of being in business—generating invoices (business value-add—indirect), designing future products and services (business value-add—future), and generating the payroll (business value-add— administrative). While some activities simply have to be done in order for the firm to exist, these types of activities do not generate revenue from today's customers. Business value-add activity costs come directly out of profit.

Even when an activity is inherently value-adding, it contains some form of business value-add and waste. Paperwork abounds, absorbing time and dollars for which the final customer won't reimburse the firm. Every activity also contains some element of waste—one can always find a better way of performing an activity. This fact drives the continuous improvement movement, one that the VCMS embraces.

Business value-added activities are the ones that should be targeted when the firm is attempting to improve its profitability through process redesign. Since these activities, or portions of activities, come directly out of profit, finding better ways to do them or eliminating them altogether drives profit improvement. However, not all business value-added activities are created equal. They differ in terms of how vital they are to the long-run success of the organization.

BVA$_I$—Indirect Customer Support

Business value-add indirect (BVA$_I$) is a category of activities that indirectly touch the customer. They are not part of the value proposition of the firm, but they are tied to the customer transaction. One of the most common of these activities is the generation of an invoice for an order. The customer expects an invoice, but doesn't value getting it. On the other hand, if the invoice is incorrect, customers can become dissatisfied with the firm. This dissatisfaction can actually lead to the search for an alternative service or product provider.

When doing a cost analysis, it is truly amazing how many activities have at least some portion of BVA$_I$ embedded in them. Each time the firm completes a "touch" moment with the customer, BVA_I actions take place. As seen in Figure 3.1, taken from Easy Air's research study, a broad range of activities contain some element of BVA_I.

As can be seen from this example of the internal group that establishes meetings and group events, there is some level of customer service provided that is indirect to the customer but essential to the relationship of the firm with its customers. For instance, internal and external communications have no direct customer value-add assigned to it, but is seen as being 20% indirect value-add. The importance of BVA_I activities was perceived to be so important that Easy Air decided that it wanted to include BVA_I actions in its definition and analysis of value-add in the firm.

Another example of BVA_I is daily operations development and maintenance. Clearly the customer would suffer if the airline did not develop daily operational reports that are used to coordinate the timing of flights and the rotation of aircraft to various routes or maintenance. This is essential information for the smooth operations that the customer does benefit from. The customer expects that this work is done, but does not want to pay for it in their purchase transaction.

The splitting of activities across multiple classifications reflects the fact that activities are made up of tasks, or actions, that take place. While an activity can be predominantly business value-add—administrative, for instance, it may contain some tasks that indirectly touch the customer. This ability to allow for task or action level thinking without having to collect all of the data on what these tasks are is one of the strengths of the VCMS. It provides an elegant way to capture the impact of task detail without the laborious process of identifying and tracking each action taken in the firm.

So, what are some of the common activities in a firm that are predominantly BVA_I? They would include the following:

- Purchase order processing
- Preparing shipping documents
- Maintaining customer accounts
- Preparing invoices
- All coordination activities, such as scheduling

2. Activity-to-value creation category mapping

Process code	Activity description	Customer value-adding activities		Business value-adding activities		Wasted time and effort %	Total (must equal 100%)
		Directly touches the customer %	Indirectly supports customer needs %	Time spent to build future business %	Time for running the business %		
4.1.06	Develop marketing plan & strategy	0%	0%	50%	50%	0%	100%
4.1.06	Evaluate & execute proposals and promotions	10%	5%	40%	35%	10%	100%
4.1.06	Evaluate & attend tradeshows, forums, fam trips	15%	0%	80%		5%	100%
4.1.06	Advertising & collateral development		5%	60%	30%	5%	100%
4.1.06	Lead generation & sales tools development		5%	60%	30%	5%	100%
4.1.06	Sales calls and media inquiries	10%	5%	60%	20%	5%	100%
4.1.06	Daily operations development & maintenance		15%	20%	60%	5%	100%
8.6.5	Reporting of business (field sales reports, arr/dep, rev)			35%	60%	5%	100%
4.1.06	Special projects			15%	80%	5%	100%

4.1.06	Competitive research/industry knowledge			95%		5%	100%
4.1.06	Administrative duties (calls, correspondence, tix)			35%	60%	5%	100%
4.1.06	Collateral upkeep & fulfillment	10%		30%	55%	5%	100%
8.6.5	Internal & external communication		20%	50%	20%	10%	100%
8.6.5	Customer service	30%	10%	60%		0%	100%
4.1.06	Systems analysis & development		10%	40%	50%	0%	100%
4.1.06	Team training & development		10%	30%	60%	0%	100%
8.5.3	Team supervision/mentoring			50%	50%	0%	100%
8.3.3	Recruit/Hire			40%	60%	0%	100%
10.1.1	Maintain budget			45%	50%	5%	100%
4.1.06	Establish & maintain goals			50%	50%	0%	100%

NOTE: Each of the rows should sum to 100% of the available time and effort the activity consumes.

Figure 3.1. Business value-add—indirect.

- Internal customer tracking and analysis
- Order entry
- Order fulfillment, such as picking the ordered items
- Return processing
- Complaint processing
- Order taking

What all of these types of activities have in common is the fact that if they are done poorly, the customer is directly impacted. Clearly these activities do not make up part of the product or service value proposition, but they can impact customer satisfaction with the transactions that they undertake with the firm.

BVA_I, then, is tied to the satisfaction metrics that a firm collects. When customers are satisfied with the results of a transaction with the firm, it usually means that the BVA_I element of the firm's activities have gone so smoothly that they are invisible to the customer. Since satisfaction has long-term implications for the continuation of a customer relationship, tying to the customer's loyalty to the firm, BVA_I actions are critical to long-term survival and growth. That being said, they do not warrant direct payment by the customer, who simply expects them to be done quickly and correctly.

If a service logic approach[2] is taken to the customer relationship, many of these activities could be classified as part of the responsiveness or quality of service component of the value proposition. This fact underscores why some of the activities in Figure 3.1 have some value-add even when the function of setting operational meetings and requirements itself would probably be dominantly classified as administrative work. There is value-add in all corners of the organization and a surprising number of places where BVA_I occurs. Whenever an action is one step removed from directly touching the customer, it is a BVA_I action.

BVA_F—Building the Future of the Business

One of the most important things for a firm's long-term survival is its ability to create new products and services and to sell these new products and services to new and existing customers. What is fascinating about business value-add—future (BVA$_F$) activities, then, is that they are forward-looking but actually are not valued by a customer buying today's products. If you just made a decision to buy a new computer, for instance, you are not happy (nor factor into your price) the fact that a new model is released the next day. BVA$_F$ activities can actually make today's customers feel as though they've been cheated out of extra value because they made a purchase decision—they draw the entire purchase decision into question.

A company, though, always needs to be looking to the next transaction, or the next purchase of its goods and services. While today's sales may be the source of celebration, once the confetti settles it's time to get back to work to generate new products and new sales. So, even though today's customers won't pay for BVA$_F$ actions or activities, future customers will. In cutting costs, then, BVA$_F$ activities may seem discretionary, but they are actually essential to long-term survival and growth. Companies that fail to plan for the future will find themselves out of touch with the market and in a losing situation.

Once again returning to Easy Air, we see in Figure 3.2 that a marketing department has a heavy component of BVA$_F$ in its core activities. For instance, strategic planning is essential for the long-term survival of Easy Air, so it is deemed to be 95% BVA$_F$. Clearly today's customers don't really care if a company does any strategic planning at all, but if the company is to be around for tomorrow's customers it is a vital activity.

What are some of the activities that take place in a firm that are predominantly BVA$_F$ in nature? They would include the following:

- Strategic planning
- Pricing analysis
- Customer research
- Product development
- Basic research
- Proposal development
- Marketing analysis
- Advertising
- Marketing research
- Design for manufacturability

2. Activity-to-value creation category mapping

Process code	Activity description	Customer value-adding activities		Business value-adding activities			Total (must equal 100%)
		Directly touches the customer %	Indirectly supports customer needs %	Time spent to build future business %	Time for running the business %	Wasted time and effort %	
1.3	Strategic planning (meetings)			95%		5%	100%
1.3	Plan execution—fare sale planning; meetings			90%		10%	100%
8.5.3	Staff meetings				95%	5%	100%
1.3	Data pulling/research			85%	5%	10%	100%
1.3	Ad hoc analysis/reporting			85%	5%	10%	100%
1.3	Weekly reporting				100%		100%
1.3	Monthly reporting				100%		100%
4.4.2	Gov't bidding & administration			45%	45%	10%	100%
1.3	Report design			30%	65%	5%	100%
8.5.3	Administration/team management				90%	10%	100%
8.6.5	RR monthly report assembly				95%	5%	100%
8.6.5	Distribution				100%		100%

NOTE: Each of the rows should sum to 100% of the available time and effort the activity consumes.

Figure 3.2. *Business value-add—future.*

- Process improvement efforts, such as lean management
- Customer focus groups
- Customer satisfaction studies

This list could be much longer. A well-run organization is always look-ing forward, so it spends a significant amount of its time and resources making sure it has the next new product or service offering ready to hit the market when the timing is deemed right. In fact, it is common knowledge that firms such as Sony and Apple plan for their own products' obsoles-cence and replacement by new models out six or seven iterations. Since it takes time to bring new products into the market, the firm has to be con-stantly looking forward to ensure that it remains viable in the marketplace.

BVA_P, then, is definitely value-adding from the shareholder perspec-tive. Investors in a firm are buying its future cash flows, not its current or past ones. While the VCMS focuses on customers, the management of the firm has to keep the expectations of all of its stakeholders in mind. Today's customers may generate today's revenues and profits, but tomor-row's products and services are the basis for investors to provide vital working capital to the firm.

Finally, unfortunately for many companies, financial accounting often categorizes BVA_F actions and activities as discretionary. This approach means that when times get tight, these activities may be curtailed, increas-ing current profitability. But this increase in current profits comes at a high cost—tomorrow's survival and possible success. These activities are hardly discretionary for a firm focused on its future growth. The VCMS does a better job of isolating those factors that drive future growth. These BVA_F activities are second in line for protection when cost cutting takes place. Removing costs should come from administrative and waste activities first and foremost, with the savings reinvested in current value-add and future value-add activities. While every activity can always be done more effectively, planning for the future is not an option—it is essential to business survival.

BVA_A—Administration, or Feeding the Beast

One of the functions most poorly contained in many companies is its administrative work. Reflecting tasks that focus on internal communication and coordination, business value-add—administrative (BVA_A) activities do not add value to the company in the short- or long-term. No customer is going to pay a company for holding its meetings or for the reports management requests. While some level of administrative work, such as processing payroll, is important to the individuals in the firm, these activities never create value and can, in fact, become value destroyers.

Much of the work that takes place to coordinate and communicate across the value chain falls into the administrative category. In fact, supply chain partners can be a source of this nonvalue-added category of work. This fact underscores why it is important for the term customer to mean the final consumer—value chain partners may require work that doesn't in any way impact the final value contained in a product or service. These activities may generate cost and reduce profits—they can never grow the top line. When negotiating with trading partners, then, a company should identify and work to eliminate unnecessary BVA_A activities from the relationship.

The more complex or bureaucratic an organization is the larger percentage of its resources may be used for internal coordination activities. It is also an area where waste can become rampant because BVA_A activities are hard to measure and control. Who can really say what the importance of a single meeting is? Because it is so hard to define what the right amount of administrative work is from an internal perspective, companies are turning to benchmarking to identify best practice in administrative work.

As can be seen in Figure 3.3 taken from Easy Air, areas such as the corporate tax department are predominantly BVA_A in nature. The company has to pay its taxes, and can gain profitability from a good tax strategy, but no real value is created for customers with this work. As can be seen, though, there is some future value add in these activities because good tax positioning has a major impact on future profitability.

In this list of tax-driven activities, research has a significant amount of future value-add while filling out and filing liquor tax forms is deemed to be purely administrative. Compliance activities, while essential if the firm is to stay in business, never create value for today's or tomorrow's customers.

| | | 2. Activity-to-value creation category mapping | | | | | |
| | | Customer value-adding activities | | Business value-adding activities | | | |
Process code	Activity description	Directly touches the customer %	Indirectly supports customer needs %	Time spent to build future business %	Time for running the business %	Wasted time and effort %	Total (must equal 100%)
8.6.5	Meetings & administration			40%	45%	15%	100%
8.4.4	Training			80%	18%	2%	100%
6.3.2.14	Downtime					100%	100%
10.5.1	Federal income tax compliance			10%	85%	5%	100%
10.5.1	Federal excise tax compliance				99%	1%	100%
10.5.1	State tax compliance (income)			10%	88%	2%	100%
10.5.1	State tax compliance (property)			10%	85%	5%	100%
10.5.1	State tax compliance (sales & use)			10%	85%	5%	100%
10.5.1	State tax compliance (liquor)				99%	1%	100%
10.5.1	State tax compliance (fuel)			10%	80%	10%	100%
10.5.4	Federal tax audits & controversy				40%	60%	100%
10.5.4	State tax audits & controversy				60%	40%	100%

Figure 3.3. Business value-add—administrative (continued).

2. Activity-to-value creation category mapping

Process code	Activity description	Customer value-adding activities		Business value-adding activities			Total (must equal 100%)
		Directly touches the customer %	Indirectly supports customer needs %	Time spent to build future business %	Time for running the business %	Wasted time and effort %	
10.5.2	Tax planning & tax minimization projects			80%	15%	5%	100%
10.5.1	Federal tax research			50%	48%	2%	100%
10.5.4	Governmental affairs & legislative issues			80%	18%	2%	100%
10.5.4	Tax consulting with other departments			50%	45%	5%	100%
10.5.1	Financial accounting for taxes				97%	3%	100%
8.4.4	Reading tax periodicals			70%	30%	0%	100%
8.7	Southwest spirit events			70%	30%	0%	100%
8.4.4	Supervising & coaching			80%	20%	0%	100%
10.1.1	Department budgeting			79%	20%	1%	100%
10.5.6	Manage tax systems & automation efforts			60%	39%	1%	100%

NOTE: Each of the rows should sum to 100% of the available time and effort the activity consumes.

Figure 3.3. Business value-add—administrative (continued).

The goal in the BVA$_A$ arena, then, is to do these tasks as efficiently as possible. When cost cutting is needed, these are the first activities that should be targeted. In fact, many companies today outsource these activities to firms that specialize in them because they have found this is the most efficient way to get the tasks done. Some companies outsource their payroll function, for instance, to firms such as EDS that specialize in payroll activities. Given the complexity in complying to all the regulations and tax laws that surround payroll, this outsourcing might make good business sense.

In other organizations, centralization of these tasks for an entire group of subunits is common. For instance, at Johnson & Johnson, all accounts payable for the corporation's many companies are processed at one central site. This allows for gains in efficiency through the use of advanced technologies that could not be justified on a subunit level. So, what are the kinds of activities or tasks that fall into administrative categories? They include the following:

- Meetings
- Reports
- Compliance work
- Tax accounting
- Financial accounting
- Accounts payable
- Accounts receivable
- Purchasing
- Payroll
- Scheduling
- Management

What all of these activities have in common is that they exist solely to keep the organization functioning. No customer, whether current or future, benefits from this work. It is even difficult to argue that any stakeholder benefits from these activities. That is why in several companies this type of work was referred to as "feeding the beast." Management drives this cost area. Management is the only party that can be said to benefit from these activities. The question is how much time and effort should go into management activities?

At one firm that had adopted team-based management approaches, the extreme impact of management methods on BVA_A levels in a firm were seen. In this bicycle manufacturing firm, four to six hours of each manager's day was spent in meetings. When did these individuals get their real work done? It was mostly done in the evenings and on weekends. The managers of the company were still held accountable for accomplishing their primary jobs, but there wasn't enough time left in the work day to get it done. This extreme case illustrates the fact that BVA_A activities can become profit destroyers quite rapidly if not aggressively managed.

Administrative functions seem to grow of their own accord. For instance, in many colleges the number of students that the campus can accommodate is capped by classroom and dorm capacity. The number of faculty, who are direct labor, is tied to the student enrollment. However, even though we observe the same numbers of students graduating and taught by the same number of faculty, we sometimes see more and more layers of administrators added to the organizations, explaining some of the observed increases in tuition.

Administrative work, even when necessary, should be contained. Growth in administrative areas should be closely monitored and examined to make sure there really is a justification for adding more personnel. Otherwise management can be caught up in the trap of spending more and more resources to manage itself. Since these activity costs come directly out of profit and will never generate a penny in revenue, they should be tightly controlled to ensure that the future of the firm is not put at risk. Feeding the beast has to be an activity constantly placed on a "diet" to lessen its impact on current and future profitability.

Summary

This chapter has looked at the various types of business value-added activities that can take place in an organization. Using examples taken from Easy Air, we identified how one specific activity can have portions of value-add, BVA_I, BVA_P, BVA_A, and waste embedded in it. In reality, this information taps the task level of an activity, but it does so without requiring the individual manager to actually lay out the details of how work is done. This innovation in data collection separates the VCMS from most activity-based cost systems that place an activity completely within either value-add or nonvalue-add categories.

For all business value-add activities, making the dollars spent stretch as far as possible is the key. Since they don't generate any revenue today, the spending can only come from one place—profit. Business value-add activities can squeeze the profit right out of a firm. They reflect management decisions and management actions that do not tie directly to the company's current value proposition.

That being said, it is important to protect many of the activities that are predominantly business value-add—future. These are activities that ensure the future viability and success of the organization, and hence are actually seen as value-adding by the firm's shareholders. Far from being discretionary in nature, BVA_F activities are the source for long-term growth and sustainability.

There are many ways that companies can contain the costs of administrative work, including outsourcing and centralization of tasks. When lean initiatives are launched, the very first place they should be focused is on BVA_A activities because these are not profit generating but rather rob the firm of its profitability. Every activity has some level of administration in it. The goal is to make this as small a portion as is feasible and still retain control of the organization.

By creating this robust categorization of business activities, the VCMS expands the knowledge created by activity analysis and process improvement programs. It also more accurately reflects the reality on the ground—what individuals really see as the costs and benefits of their activities. Having looked at this area in depth, then, let's turn our attention to waste, the profit bandit.

> *The important thing is this: to be able at any moment to sacrifice*
> *what we are for what we could become.*
>
> Charles Du Bos[3]

CHAPTER 4

A Focus on Waste: Eliminating Nonvalue-Added Activities

A man cannot be paid much for producing something which is wasted.

Henry Ford[1]

Waste is something that no human being enjoys creating. To waste resources is to potentially create a resource shortage in the future. To do work that is deemed to be wasteful is demoralizing. Waste destroys profit and current and future opportunities to create value. A company has to recognize, measure, and eliminate waste if it is to achieve its profit potential.[2] Waste occurs throughout the organization, in every activity and every function. The goal in measuring waste is to make it visible so it can be eliminated.

The Many Faces of Waste

Waste is an insidious part of every organizational activity. Every time someone has to repeat an action or undo something another person has done, waste occurs. When workers are left idle because of poor scheduling, waste occurs. And as Henry Ford suggested in the opening quote, it is difficult to pay someone for creating waste.

Figure 4.1 provides a list of many ways in which waste is created in organizations. As we saw in the Easy Air example in Chapter 3, waste can also be embedded at the task or action level. Waste occurs when there is miscommunication, so that a task is "fumbled" as it passes from one work station to another. When too much value is added to a product, waste is created. Much of the paperwork that consumes so much of the BVA_A activities in a firm is waste. So, what are the various faces of waste?

Excess complexity	Move	Queue	Defects	Unfocused processes
Redundancy	Excess variation	Idle capacity	Setup	Overproduction
"Re" anything	Inadequate training	Un-empowered workers	Fumbles/ errors	Poor communication

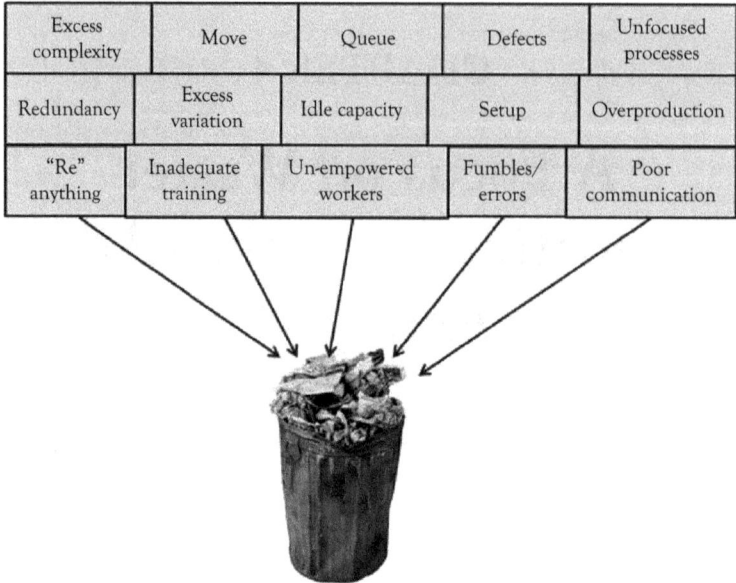

Figure 4.1. The many faces of waste.

Note that waste drops directly into a garbage can in this figure. Waste is the garbage of the organization, collecting in activity after activity. Since waste comes directly out of profit, it destroys the value of the firm. It is spending that never benefits anyone—it simply robs the profit potential of the firm.

One of the easiest ways to spot waste is to follow a piece of paper, perhaps an order to be produced, through an organization. What is seen is that waste starts to accumulate as soon as the order is launched. It can be in such simple things as the order entry activity. Let's say the order is taken by customer service clerks, who fill out all the required forms (physical waste) and then staple them together in the order they were trained to use. The order is then walked down the hall to order entry (move, a waste factor) where it is placed in the order entry clerk's in basket (queue, some more waste). Once the order entry clerk picks up the packet, it is immediately unstapled because the sheets are not in the order that the computer screens require (undo, redo, waste). The clerk then enters the information into the system and it moves on to production scheduling.

Waste would be eliminated here if the customer service representative directly entered the order detail into the computer while talking with the customer. An order receipt could be generated immediately and e-mailed to the customer, providing a touch point and getting an early lead on potential order entry errors. Waste is converted in this way into a value-add activity, namely service responsiveness. The savings can be used to further improve order entry functions or to add to the firm's value-added core. The former will potentially reduce BVA_A, which means improved profitability. The latter will promote a cycle of growth for the company. Either way, getting the waste out is essential to today's and tomorrow's profitability.

The Lean Model and VCMS

The lean management model has an overriding goal—to identify and eliminate waste from the organization wherever it occurs through a process of continuous improvement. Using process analysis techniques, teams map out the workflow for various outputs and use mapping graphics to identify the primary sources of waste. This value stream mapping documents and then directs the transformation to a lean enterprise. In discussing value stream mapping, Keyte and Locher note the following:[3]

> Though value stream mapping can identify continued opportunities to enhance value, eliminate waste, and improve flow, it is not the end, but the beginning of the journey in value stream management. In Deming terms, it is the "P" in the PDCA cycle (plan-do-check-act) … It allows a company to document, measure, and analyze a complex set of relationships as well as to plot a course to create an improved operating strategy and organizational design.

Value stream mapping can be done in both productive and support areas of the firm. At one site, the U.S. Coast Guard Finance Center (FINCEN), the accounts payable function was analyzed to identify ways to streamline the process so the organization could take greater advantage of prompt payment discounts offered by their vendors. One of the value stream maps created during this exercise is shown in Figure 4.2.

As can be seen, there were a large number of sources of error in entering vendor information. This led to delayed payments and loss of the prompt payment discount. The operation to enter vendor information was also overly complex, with the accounts payable individual having to access three

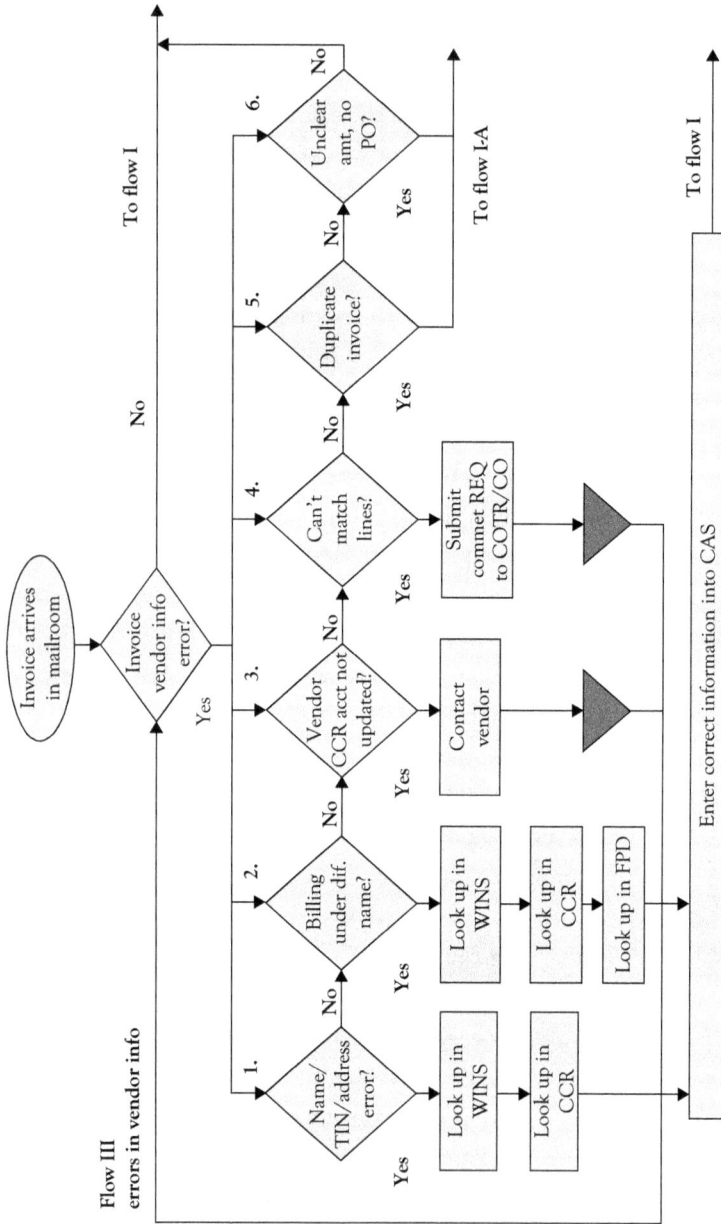

Figure 4.2. A value stream map.

major databases to complete the data entry task. Every one of the diamonds in Figure 4.2 represents waste, as does the tasks taken to remediate an error in the vendor information. This was an entire flow of wasted activities, one that cost the Coast Guard significant amount of resources and benefits.

The flow was fixed using a combination of lean and VCMS techniques. Within the first six weeks after the process was improved, the Coast Guard saw a $1 million increase in the amount of purchase discounts taken. This money was immediately put to use to provide the Coast Guard fleet with more fuel and resources to expand their mission base, a direct creation of more value for the country.

Waste in Every Activity

What we saw in Easy Air's charts was the fact that many activities have some level of waste in them. When collecting this information, employees are often hesitant to insert any waste into their responses, fearing management repercussions. But, huge improvements identified with lean management would not exist if there was not waste in every activity. The goal has to be to constantly work with the information providers so that they become more comfortable with identifying the "re's" existing in most processes.

Let's look at an activity grid from Windows, Inc. to see an example of the kind of waste that is embedded in their processes (see Figure 4.3). As you can see, every activity is noted to have some level of waste in it.

2. Activity-value assignment						
For each activity from step (1), please estimate the percentage of this effort that would be considered customer value-add (a customer would pay for it), business value-add (C, F or A), or non value-add.						
Activity description	% Customer value-add	% Business value-add: indirect	% Business value-add: future	% Business value-add: admin.	Waste	Total (must equal 100%)
Address manufacturing problems	30%	60%			10%	100%
Cost reduction/quality improvement	20%	30%	40%		10%	100%
Employee suggestions	10%	30%	30%	10%	20%	100%
New products/sizes/part numbers	50%		30%		20%	100%
Address ergonomic/safety issues	10%	50%	20%		20%	100%
Administrative requirements		50%			50%	100%
Develop future projects/ideas	30%	10%	30%		30%	100%
Supervisory responsibilities				50%	50%	100%
Attend meetings		10%	15%	35%	40%	100%

Figure 4.3. Windows, Inc. waste reporting.

Administrative reporting is perceived as 50% waste, while even 20% of the value-adding activity of supporting the development of new products is perceived as waste. This manager was very honest, probably due to the fact that he worked in product quality management function and was familiar with how this information would be deployed. In collecting this type of information employees need to understand the purpose for collecting the information and the way that this information will be used.

We can also tell something about the individual who prepared the report shown here. He clearly doesn't think much of spending his time in meetings or meeting administrative requirements. He even puts 50% waste on his supervisory responsibilities. This clearly is someone who prefers action to talking about work. That's a good fit for someone in the quality area, as is the honesty and objectivity in reporting about different aspects of his job. The information in Figure 4.3, then, is an ideal state where the individual who responded really understood the purpose of the data collection and reports objectively. It can take several iterations to gain this much trust in an organization. No one likes to admit to waste.

Structural Versus Process-Based Waste

Waste can be embedded in the structure of the organization, as we've seen here. A very top-down management structure that requires a lot of paperwork and meetings embeds significant amounts of waste in everyone's workday. Even if a meeting is productive, there are elements of waste in it. Anyone who has sat through the tedium of one PowerPoint presentation after another knows this fact. Unless a meeting is called to address a specific problem and is expected to yield concrete take-way points, it can waste a significant amount of a firm's most valuable resource—the time individuals have available to do value-adding work.

What we see in Figure 4.4 is that the structure of the organization can embed waste that constricts the flow of the value-added processes. Structural waste, then, restricts the growth of the total organization. Process-based waste, on the other hand, restricts the total amount of value the organization can create within its structural boundaries.[4]

The way in which a company is structured defines the type and amount of resources it will need to accomplish its work. This structure—the number

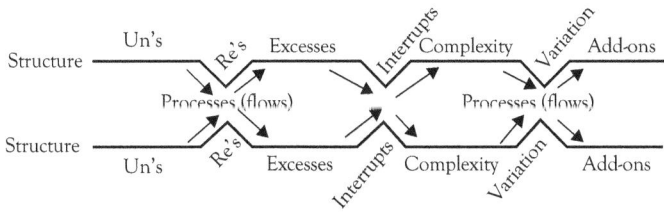

Figure 4.4. Structural versus process-based waste.

of plants, divisions, departments, or related subunits the company has as well as where they are located and how they interact—places boundaries around the value creation process. And in the same way that the structure of a garden hose constricts the amount of water that can flow through it, the structure of an organization constrains the amount of work it can do in any defined period of time.

There are three basic ways that waste is built into the structure of an organization. These permanently increase the amount of cost that is incurred when operating the system to deliver goods and services:

- There can be excess capacity in the system in total, or of specific key resources. An example here would be a machine that is "slaved" to a just-in-time cell. No matter what the true capacity of that machine is to do work, it will only be used up to the point required to balance the flow. Significant amounts of the machine's capacity can be permanently wasted. This is not to say that this "slaving" is always undesirable—it simply needs to be done with a clear understanding of its impact on long-term profitability.
- Inadequate development of the baseline capability of the people that interact within the system. If people are not trained to do a job efficiently and effectively, waste becomes rampant. Training can be a significant waste reducer.
- Unnecessary or excessive complexity in the structure and activities of the value chains that deliver specific goods and services to customers and markets. Simplifying value chains is one of the goals of value chain management. Removing steps in the value chain can remove significant amounts of embedded waste.

Process waste comes from all of the "un's," "re's," excesses, interruptions, complexity, variation, and add-on activities that constrict the flow through the structural boundaries of the organization—they are kinks in the hose of value creation. Each of these forms of waste reduces the organization's ability to create value for its customers as they reduce the flow of value creating work. Removing process-based waste allows an organization to reach the profit potential its structure allows.

The Behavioral Impact of Waste

As noted in the opening pages of this chapter, no one likes to do work that ends up being defined as waste. During one visit to a bar soap manufacturer, the impact of waste on employee morale became very visible. Each subsequent bad bar was flung more angrily into the waste bin. Sure, the soap could be reworked, but everyone knew that was not the optimal path. It angers people to see their work tossed away. It is an unusual person who doesn't prefer the satisfaction of a job well done to one that is deemed to be waste.

There are ways to make waste visible that can alert employees to the status of their efforts. At one refrigerator manufacturer, a "waste" meter was set up that noted at each stage of production what the level of waste was and how that translated into dollars of lost profit. Employees took more care in their work, not wanting to be the one to drive up the waste meter for the day. It also led to some strange behavior at the end of the line, though, as several strong men used rubber mallets to get doors into alignment so they could pass final inspection. While the intent of this activity was laudable, the doors should have been in alignment to start with.

Figure 4.5 suggests a way to think about waste and measure it to reduce its consequences. The key thing is to measure waste to make it visible, also tracking waste so that it is discovered as soon as possible in the work flow. And, as some of the Japanese models suggest, waste can be a primary source of organizational learning. Improvement in how work is done comes from understanding how waste occurs and then developing methods and techniques to eliminate it. In the beginning, there is waste everywhere, but as processes are improved, waste becomes a gem that

Envision vaste.

Learn from waste.

Identify waste wherever it's found.

Measure waste to make it visible.   *Insure*

Investigate every activity for waste.   *Tomorrow*

Negotiate to eliminate waste.

Analyze the causes of waste.

Track waste to prevent its growth.

Eliminate waste wherever it's found.

Figure 4.5. Eliminating waste: a framework for action.[5]

leads to more improvement efforts. In the pursuit of continuous improvement and Six Sigma quality levels, a company seeks out waste wherever it occurs, in an honest search for ways to eliminate it.

One final comment needs to be made. Employees are not the cause of waste—they are the key to eliminating it. Without employees, dedicated to improving the process, the goals of the organization cannot be reached. Waste elimination, then, helps to bring the organization together with a common purpose—to purge waste from every activity, action and task so that the firm can reach its profit potential.

Summary

In this chapter we've talked about the various forms that waste can take in the organization, and noted how important it is to eliminate it wherever it is found. Wasted actions can demoralize the workforce and reduce a firm's profit potential. The profit potential of a firm's set of resources is constrained by the structure of its processes and subunits. Highly bureaucratic firms are more prone to waste because of the high level of administrative work that has to be done as well as the embedded delays that take place when decisions and actions have to work their way up the chain of command before they can be undertaken. That is why an empowered workforce is so important—it helps to stop waste at the point of action, reducing its total impact on the organization.

It's important to find ways to make waste visible so that it can be acted upon. While employees are often hesitant to admit to the presence of waste in their activities, there is waste everywhere. Making employees comfortable with the fact that identifying waste is actually an opportunity to improve performance rather than the source of punishment is a critical step in making the VCMS a reliable basis for taking action. If everyone begins to see waste as a gem that leads to continuous improvement and learning, it becomes much easier to get this information from them.

Waste takes many forms, including excess capacity, "re's," "un's," and any number of other sources. Value stream mapping helps identify waste at the task level, but cannot always be undertaken. The VCMS allows managers to pinpoint waste and focus attention on areas deemed to have the most waste. Decisions can then be made whether to expend the resources required to complete a value stream map or to instead use brainstorming or employee expertise to isolate and eliminate the identified waste.

Waste robs an organization of its future value-creating potential. Because the VCMS allows for waste in every activity, it differs from existing activity analysis practices that only isolate entire activities that are waste. Waste takes place at the task or action level, and that is where it needs to be addressed. It is everyone's job to find and eliminate waste so a firm can reach its profit potential.

In formal logic, a contradiction is a signal of defeat; but in the evolution of real knowledge it marks the first step in progress toward a victory.

Alfred North Whitehead[6]

CHAPTER 5

Multiplying Value

*Knowledge is the only instrument of production that is not subject to
diminishing returns.*

John Maurice Clark[1]

What makes the value-based cost management system (VCMS) different
from traditional accounting models is that it allows for the fact that value
grows within an organization. Traditional accounting only supports linear
transformations in the accounting equation—add, subtract, multiply, and
divide. There is no room for value creation in this equation, not unless it
adheres to very strict mathematical rules of development. In developing a
VCMS, the focus turns to those actions a company performs that create
profitable growth. In addition, a VCMS is strategic in nature—current
information is used to create a focus on those activities and outcomes that
help grow the top line of the business.

In this chapter we focus on the multiplicative relationship between
the revenues earned by customer value-added efforts and the resources
consumed in the company to deliver this level of value-add—the revenue
multiplier. The resulting value-add revenue to value-add costs ratio reflects
the fact that a high growth curve can be created by investing resources in
activities that customers value. The goal is to better understand the dynamics of the VCMS that separates it from traditional accounting. It is a marketing view on the accounts of the company, one that allows for the growth
of value creation through careful investments in the areas customers value.

Comparing Revenues to Value-Add

One of the first things the VCMS does is to capture data on the value-
added components of a company's value profile. Based on customer data,
the VCMS starts where product development and marketing start—by

understanding exactly what a customer wants and expects from the products and services a firm provides. VCMS then uses the fact that revenues
represent the sum total of the firm's value proposition to create a usable
accounting structure for the firm. Revenues are the key linchpin that
makes the VCMS work.

What is the essence of comparing revenues to value-add? It is transforming the desires of customers away from vague references to concepts such as "prefer" and "prefer highly," to concrete trade-offs, which
are, in reality, at the heart of consumer behavior. Two steps need to
be taken, then, to make marketing data-friendly from the accounting
perspective. First, the list of value attributes needs to be generated for
a product. Depending on the type of the market the firm operates in,
this list may consist anywhere from just a few to many attributes that
capture the value proposition the customer really considers when making a purchase.

The customer value attribute weightings for a small farm implement
manufacturer in Italy provide a good example of the weights making up a
set of value attributes (see Figure 5.1). We see here that technical reliability
and performance are critical components of customer value (35%). Price
as a proxy measure for standard functionality and life cycle costs comes in
a close second, noting the fact that there is a 34% commodity component
to the value structure of the firm. Getting immediate help to customers
who experience a breakdown during planting or harvest accounts for the
remaining 31% of the total value delivered by Frangor's products.

Attribute	Market weight	Revenue equivalent (in million $'s)	Value-added cost (in million $'s)	Value multiplier
Technical reliability	25%	$3.72	$0.37	10.1
Price	19%	$2.83	$0.33	8.6
Service reliability	17%	$2.53	$0.22	11.5
Life cycle cost	15%	$2.23	$0.17	13.1
Customer assistance	14%	$2.09	$0.06	34.8
Technical performance	10%	$1.49	$0.02	74.5
Total	100%	$14.89	$1.17	12.7

Figure 5.1. Frangor manufacturing.

The value multipliers for this firm are high. At the time of this project, the customer satisfaction data indicated that customers were satisfied with the technical reliability of the product, but customer satisfaction was low on other value attribute dimensions. For example, customers had to wait to get repairs made, causing significant problems for the farmer during critical growing seasons. Providing timely customer service is a critical dimension of customer value in this market. For example, it is so important that Caterpillar, Inc. focuses on timely customer service as the key aspect of its customer service, using a worldwide distribution network that guarantees a customer will be back up and running within 24 hours of the initial call.[2]

Once the customer data are collected and value attributes and their importance in the customer value profile are established and examined to make sure they add up to 100%, the linkage to revenue can be created. The percentage of total value is translated to the percentage of total revenue earned by the product. Looking at the revenue equivalent line we see the weighted average of the value attribute in general is multiplied by the total revenue that product is predicted to generate. These *revenue equivalents* provide critical data for the VCMS calculations.

Revenue equivalents are the vital linkage between the accounting and marketing functions in the firm. By providing a baseline number that can be used to analyze the marketing data from a financial perspective, the revenue equivalent provides a common language that everyone can understand and apply to making effective decisions that reflect customer preferences. This is one of the two critical innovations in the VCMS model.

The Role of Value Multipliers

Once the revenue equivalents have been developed, attention turns to the cost data. Using the methods described in earlier chapters, managers are asked to define activities performed by their business unit. Added to the traditional activity analysis that underlies all activity-based approaches to cost management are several key steps:

1. The activity is assessed to determine its percentage of value-add, BVA_I, BVA_P, BVA_A, and waste or nonvalue-add.
2. The budget for the department is then "blown out" across the activities by percentage of value-add, business value-add, and waste.

3. For those activities that are determined to have some percentage of value-add, the manager is asked to assign this dollar amount of value-added activities across the value attributes defined by the customer.
4. Once this percentage assignment has been completed for attributes, the dollars of value-add are weighted by the attribute percentage to get the dollars of value-add by attribute.

As we saw earlier, by ensuring that 100% of an activity goes to value-add, business value-add, or waste, we can take the dollars assigned to the activity and divide them across these categories. Once we have a dollar amount assigned to the value-added activities, we then assign 100% of this amount to one or more of the attributes. This provides us with a value-added cost per attribute by activity. The first step in doing this is to break out the value-add activities (only) on the attributes as can be seen in Figure 5.2 taken from Windows, Inc.

Now that we have the percentage of the value-add activity broken down by attribute, we transform these weightings into dollars. The entire budget has already been subdivided by value-add, business value-add, and waste. What we do now is take only the value-added dollars and apply the weightings in Figure 5.2 to get the value-added dollars by attribute. The results of this analysis are shown in Figure 5.3 in two parts illustrating both the mapping to the value-added versus nonvalue-added categories as well as the mapping to the value attributes themselves.

This process is completed for every manager or targeted individual within the company. The total for each of the value attributes would then be developed, providing the total dollars per value attribute.

Creating the Value Multipliers

Having collected the revenue equivalent and cost data by value attribute, now the multipliers can be calculated. Basically, when we develop a value multiplier we take the revenue equivalents for a specific value attribute and divide them by the value-added costs that have been assigned to each attribute. For instance, let's say that the total dollars assigned to the basic product for a window by customers equals $350 million in revenue

3. Activity to value attribute weighting

For each activity you noted to be value-adding, please assign the percentage of that value that corresponds to one or more of the value attributes.

Value-adding activity	Price (e.g., Basic product)	Options (color / grilles)	Appearance	Brand	Warranty/ durability	Sizes available	Responsiveness of company	Quality of service	Total (must be 100%)
Address manufacturing problems		10%	40%	10%	40%				100%
Cost reduction/quality improvement	20%	30%			20%		30%		100%
Employee suggestions		20%	30%		20%		30%		100%
New products/sizes/part numbers	30%	50%					20%		100%
Address ergonomic/safety issues	30%			50%				20%	100%
N/A									0%
Develop future projects/ideas		10%	20%	30%		0.2	20%		100%
N/A									0%

Figure 5.2. Value attribute weightings.

4. Activity cost estimates by value creation categories.

Activity description	Activity costs	Budget $525,000					
		Value-added cost	Business value-add indirect	Business value-add future	Business value-add administration	Waste	Total
Address manufacturing problems	$201,923	$60,577	$121,154	$–	$–	$20,192	$201,923
Cost reduction/quality improvement	$80,769	$16,154	$24,231	$32,308	$–	$8,077	$80,769
Employee suggestions	$18,173	$1,817	$5,452	$5,452	$1,817	$3,635	$18,173
New products/sizes/part numbers	$30,288	$15,144	$–	$9,087	$–	$6,058	$30,288
Address ergonomic/safety issues	$32,308	$3,231	$16,154	$6,462	$–	$6,462	$32,308
Administrative requirements	$26,250	$–	$13,125	$–	$–	$13,125	$26,250
Delelop future projects/ideas	$72,692	$21,808	$7,269	$21,808	$–	$21,808	$72,692
Supervisory responsibilities	$36,346	$–	$–	$–	$18,173	$18,173	$36,346
Attend meetings	$26,250	$–	$2,625	$3,938	$9,188	$10,500	$26,250
Totals	$525,000	$118,731	$190,010	$79,053	$29,178	$108,029	$525,000

Value-added activity	Price (e.g., Basic product)	Options (color/grilles)	Appearance	Brand	Warranty/ durability	Sizes available	Responsiveness of company	Quality of service	Total
Address manufacturing problems	$–	$6,058	$24,231	$6,058	$24,231	$–	$–	$–	$60,577
Cost reduction/quality improvement	$3,231	$4,846	$–		$3,231	$–	$4,846	$–	$16,154
Employee suggestions	$–	$363	$545	$–	$363	$–	$545	$–	$1,817
New products/sizes/part numbers	$4,543	$7,572	$–	$–	$–	$–	$3,029	$–	$15,144
Address ergonomic/ safety issues	$969	$–	$–	$1,615		$–	$–	$646	$3,231
N/A	$–	$–	$–	$–	$–	$–	$–	$–	$–
Delelop future projects/ ideas	$–	$2,181	$4,362	$6,542		$4,362	$4,362	$–	$21,808
N/A	$–	$–	$–	$–	$–	$–	$–	$–	$–
N/A	$–	$–	$–	$–	$–	$–	$–	$–	$–
Totals	$8,743	$21,020	$29,138	$14,215	$27,825	$4,362	$12,782	$646	$118,731

Figure 5.3. Dollars per value attribute.

dollars. The basic costs for this attribute from the surveys collected are $125 million. What is the value multiplier?

$$\frac{\text{Revenue equivalent for price} \quad \$350 \text{ million}}{\text{Total cost for price attribute} \quad \$125 \text{ million}} = 2.8 \text{ value multiplier}$$

What does this mean? It says that for every $3.50 of revenue earned for selling a basic window, it costs $1.25 in value-adding costs to produce that window in its basic form. The $125 million investment in basic features, then, multiplies to create $350 million in revenue. This means that $0.357 of cost is incurred to earn $1 of revenue, or 35.7% of each revenue dollar earned due to price is used up in value-added costs. Since the price of the basic product reflects the firm's competitive market structure, one would expect a relatively low value multiplier. Why? It occurs because the market is constantly driving down the price earned on commodity products. Now that we know how to create a value multiplier, how do we interpret them? Let's turn to a discussion of high versus low multipliers.

High, Low, and In-between Metrics

What we saw with Frangor is that there can be very high multipliers and very poor overall performance for the firm. For convenience purposes, we will deal with high, low, and intermediate revenue/value multipliers, but they actually exist on a continuum from very small to very large. That being said, interpreting the revenue/value multipliers requires integrating value multiplier data with customer satisfaction data and other metrics measuring performance of the firm. This is especially true for high multipliers.

Low revenue/value multipliers (between 0 and 5) are more straightforward to understand. When a firm spends too many resources providing specific components of the value profile relative to customer willingness to pay, its multipliers end up being low. The more commoditized the market, the lower the overall multipliers for a product or service will be, signaling the profit pressure inherent in a cost-based strategy. Low multipliers suggest that even though the value attribute may be important, the firm is spending too much of its revenue meeting the specific category of value.

Using Impact Communications, we now can apply the 20% value-added rule to transform the data that was originally collected into one that reflects the total VCMS approach. This is being done to illustrate how different value multipliers can be found within customer segments even when the firm has a healthy value multiplier of five (see Figure 5.4). Again, this is for illustration purposes only. It is likely the true results at Impact would have been different, especially given the poor performance of the firm at the time of the study.[3]

In the Impact Communications case we identified three sets of market segments: Publicity, Marketing Service, and Strategy clients. Let's first look at the Publicity clients. In this segment, all of the value multipliers are less than 5 except for the placements quantity. Here we know, though, that the high multiplier signals a problem, because this category of client only wanted the placements activity—other attributes were not valued highly. So, the high multiplier for placements quantity combined with the satisfaction data signals to us that this might be a competitive weakness for Impact Communications.

When we look at the Marketing Services clients, we see three multipliers higher than 5—placements quantity, knowledge of the business, and results merchandising. Since these clients were happy with Impact across the board, these are competitive strengths in this segment. Impact may need to shift some of its spending on value-add activities to more closely align with the revenue equivalents, which define where value is created, but in general they are doing well with the client.

In the Strategy client segment, data indicates that these clients do not want any placements activity to take place—they have come to the firm for strategy advice. This means every dollar spent on placements is waste within this segment. Since no value is assigned, the multiplier can't even be calculated. They are happy with the research done, as well as the creativity brought to bear on their problems, accounting for the high multipliers. That being said, we see more effort could be directed toward improving results merchandising as well as knowledge of the business.

Three different segments with very different expectations and results are represented in this example. As can be found in any company that serves different customer segments, a generic approach to serving these very different groups can be deadly. Since the data was forced a bit in

Publicity clients:				
Attribute	Value weighting	Revenue equivalent	Value-added dollars (20% of total spend)	Value multiplier
Placements quantity	60.0%	$9,540.00	$782.28	12.2
Creative/proactive	15.0%	$2,385.00	$702.78	3.4
Strategy/brand	5.0%	$795.00	$861.78	0.9
Knowledge of business	10.0%	$1,590.00	$241.68	6.6
Reputation	5.0%	$795.00	$222.60	3.6
Results merchandising	5.0%	$795.00	$368.88	2.2
Total	100.0%	$15,900.00	$3,180.00	5.0

Marketing services clients:				
Attribute	Value weighting	Revenue equivalent	Value-added dollars (20% of total spend)	Value multiplier
Placements quantity	30.0%	$1,590.00	$260.76	6.1
Creative/proactive	10.0%	$530.00	$234.26	2.3
Strategy/brand	20.0%	$1,060.00	$287.26	3.7
Knowledge of business	20.0%	$1,060.00	$80.56	13.2
Reputation	5.0%	$265.00	$74.20	3.6
Results merchandising	15.0%	$795.00	$122.96	6.5
Total	100.0%	$5,300.00	$1,060.00	5.0

Strategy clients:				
Attribute	Value weighting	Revenue equivalent	Value-added dollars (20% of total spend)	Value multiplier
Placements quantity	0.0%	$0.00	$39.36	#DIV/0!
Creative/proactive	20.0%	$160.00	$35.36	4.5
Strategy/brand	60.0%	$480.00	$43.36	11.1
Knowledge of business	5.0%	$40.00	$12.16	3.3
Reputation	10.0%	$80.00	$11.20	7.1
Results merchandising	5.0%	$40.00	$18.56	2.2
Total	100.0%	$800.00	$160.00	5.0

Figure 5.4. Impact communications value multipliers.

this example, v...
average value-added... n't take the results much further than to note that the
details of how well a sp... all the segments can be the same while the actual
different. It is important to... segment's needs are being met can be quite
get a true feel for how well the... te the value multipliers by segment to
poorly, the VCMS analysis will help... doing. If a segment is performing
viding guidance on how best to redirec... e the underlying causes, pro-
unique requirements. ...s to meet the segment's

The Strategic Implications of Revenue/Value Multipliers

Revenue/value multipliers serve as strategic signals of where a c...
is doing a good job meeting customer value requirements and w...
there might be weaknesses in the product/service bundle provided to
customers. The strategic nature of the value multipliers is what makes
them so important for a firm looking to improve its long-term performance. Since customer value requirements change over time as does the
degree of competition, it is important for firms to collect and track customer value data on an ongoing basis to ensure that spending and activity
within the firm change as preferences or competition changes. The check
on the alignment of internal spending with external demands is critical
for keeping a firm one step ahead of the competition.

The information on strong value multipliers combined with good
metrics on customer satisfaction data provides a signal to marketing that
it should emphasize this value attribute when acquiring new customers.
If a firm is successful at delivering on a specific value attribute that it is
getting high multiples of payback for its effort, it is clear it is a strategic
advantage for the firm. On the other hand, if the multiplier is high but
satisfaction is low, this might be a valuable signal that the firm has to
redirect resources to better serving the customer.

The value of the VCMS, then, lies in its ability to transform the static,
historical cost data normally provided in a firm into an action-oriented,
strategically focused information source that links together the internal
efforts of the firm to create value with the market's actual assessment of
the success of these efforts. When facing a question of where to focus the

next dollar of spending to meet customer needs, the valu... ultipliers can provide vital information to make this decision. Put... ne money where customers are underserved is a way to increas... competitive strength of the organization, helping to focus its ...siness. on those activities and outcomes that will grow the top line ...gy, it may find out through the

If a firm is pursuing a low-co...fferentiated itself in some aspect of VCMS analysis that it actua...uld be used to improve the firm's com- customer value creation ...et. Since managers often have an imperfect petitive position in ...g of customer value, having a tool that helps or obsolete un... weaknesses of their products and services from an identify st... ve is crucial for long-term success. Simple in concept exter...information, value multipliers are the basis for gaining and ...g a competitive advantage in the global marketplace.
h.

Summary

In this chapter attention has focused on the concept of a revenue/value multiplier. Derived by comparing the revenue equivalent dollars to the value-added dollars required to deliver that level of value, multipliers provide strategic signals of where a firm is doing well and where it faces competitive risks. Starting with a description of how the value-added dollars are derived, the chapter emphasized the fact that multipliers vary by customer segment—one size does not fit all.

To simplify the discussion we've treated revenue/value multipliers as if they fall into one of three categories—low-, mid-, or high-range—even though in reality the multipliers exist on a continuum.[4] Mid-range multipliers, which reflect a roughly five-to-one relationship between value-added dollars and revenue equivalents, are on average the norm for a profitable company. Considering the individual attributes, the mid-range multipliers can be perceived to be "about right" in terms of the effort-to-reward relationship for the firm. Low multipliers mean that the firm is overspending to deliver on a specific attribute. The more commodity in nature an attribute or product is, the lower its multiplier is going to be. This is an unavoidable fact of the competitive marketplace. When multipliers are low, a firm should be looking to ways to differentiate itself in the market place. Since profit improvements are closely linked to top-line performance, pursuing a growth strategy is essential to long-run survival of the firm.

High multipliers present a quandary for the VCMS, one that can only be resolved by integrating VCMS analysis with the customer satisfaction data. If a value multiplier is high and customers are very satisfied with the firm's performance, it signals a competitive advantage for the firm. If the multiplier is high, though, and satisfaction is low, then the firm has a competitive weakness that could lead to long-term challenges in the market. In this regard, then, the VCMS has to not only link marketing and accounting data but also employ other metrics used to measure and assess the external success of the firm.

> *In order to maintain credibility with the customer, the people from the customer-centric global services business…must be on the side of the customer in the buyer–seller transaction.*[5]

CHAPTER 6

Implementing a Value-Based Cost Management System— Part I: Scoping the Project

The person who moves a mountain
begins by carrying away small stones.
Chinese Proverb[1]

One of the most challenging parts of any project is developing enthusiasm in the organization—the willingness to embrace change. Implementing a value-based cost management system (VCMS) is no exception. A diverse group of people need to be convinced of the value the new information embedded in the VCMS can bring to the organization. Often starting as a drive to develop a common language across the firm, the VCMS provides all of the benefits of activity-based implementations plus much more. So what is the path to implementation? It is similar to that for all major change projects, as we will outline in this chapter and the next.

Identifying the Need

Not every organization can benefit from a system such as the VCMS. If the company already uses one of the modern management tools, though, adding VCMS to the mix is an obvious next step in bringing the customer into the organization in a more formal way. For instance, if the company is already using process management, it is a relatively easy step to add the activity analysis to the process management structure. Relatedly, if the firm already uses activity-based costing, adding the VCMS categories and process framework is a logical extension of the existing processes and database.

How does one identify the need for a VCMS, then? It starts with the recognition that while the firm may state that it is customer-driven, there is often little understanding of what customer value means between different functions in the firm. For example, communication between finance/accounting and marketing might be bumpy and fraught with conflict if they base their decisions on different understandings of customer value and customer profitability. Under the VCMS, every customer could be a valuable customer if the internal spending on delivering on the value attributes that customer desires is disciplined and validated by external market measures.

What may be some of the signals that could suggest that a company would benefit if it implemented a VCMS? The indicators include the following:

- Marketing and finance are in disagreement about the customers and their value to the company.
- Customers are not loyal to the firm's products/services.
- Customer complaints suggest that the firm is not delivering on its value proposition.
- Individuals across the organization seem to differ in the language and meaning they use when discussing customers and their value requirements.
- A generic strategy is pursued even though there might be opportunities for customer segmentation.
- New product launches don't reach their profit potential.
- Administration seems to grow while the company itself is stagnant.
- Across-the-board cost cutting fails to deliver promised savings, instead shrinking the revenue line.
- Process initiatives seem to be unfocused, failing to put the customer first.
- Internal definitions are used for value-add.
- New product launches struggle to build in the voice of the customer.
- Activities are classified as purely value-add or nonvalue-add, leading to political battles as individual departments seek to justify their existence.
- Value attributes are seen merely as marketing jargon—they are not built into the language of the organization.

This list could go on, but its general thrust is clear. When the finance/accounting system is out of sync with the information demands of marketing and strategy, politics takes over and internal strife builds. In all of this, the voice of the customer can be lost, leading to potential losses of customers and entire dissatisfied segments of customers, as we saw at Impact Communications. When value-added is internally defined, it is much more challenging to systematically integrate customer value in understanding the way the firm uses its resources. And, when value-add and nonvalue-add are the only terms used to define internal activities, the ability to understand the various levels of waste and business value-add—future is compromised. Firms benefit greatly when a precise language is used if they are to truly become customer-centered.

Finding Your Champion

The need for implementing a VCMS has now been established, but that is just the starting point. Because implementing a VCMS is a cross-functional project, it really needs the CEO to be the project champion. Failing that, a cross-functional team of champions needs to be established to ensure that different functional areas work together and specifically that marketing works with finance to agree on customer value requirements in a way that is useful for the financial/accounting analysis. Since marketing and finance are traditionally serving different purposes in the firm, it is important that both functions clearly understand the benefits that can come from working together. The VCMS initiative begins, and ends, with putting the customer first.

What are the characteristics of a good project champion? The list of characteristics would include the following:

- Places top priority on meeting customer expectations
- Has a cross-functional mindset
- Understands both the marketing data and accounting data and their respective approaches
- Is good at getting diverse groups to work together
- Has enough "power" to ensure that agreements are reached

- Has the backing of top management if they are not part of the VCMS initiative
- Possesses good communication skills
- Is adept at the politics of the organization to help avoid stonewalling
- Is respected by both marketing and finance managers
- Has a positive reputation as a change agent
- Possesses good presentation skills to communicate the nature of the project to all affected managers.

These qualities are essential for making a cross-functional project such as the implementation of VCMS a success. The project champion has to be respected across the organization, so that people trust that the information they provide will be used only for its stated purpose—getting all eyes focused on the customer. If the individual has been involved earlier in successful projects such as process management or activity-based costing implementations, this is a major plus because the champion becomes both respected as a change agent and has a track record of delivering on promises.

Having identified the champion of the project, it is now time to set up the project team.

The Project Team

The project team needs to be cross-functional in nature and consist of individuals who are respected across the organization for their communication and analytical skills. The project team collects the data that is used to develop the VCMS and also puts in place a sustainable reporting system that can support the use of the VCMS moving forward. Since this is equivalent to creating a new control tool, the team members have to be sensitive to the politics involved in putting new measures in place in their organization.

As can be seen in Figure 6.1, the team should include managers from the key affected areas. It also needs to include individuals with computer expertise if the data is going to be collected easily the first time and the subsequent system that is developed for ongoing reporting is to be elegant and easy to use. While the implementations of the VCMS to date have

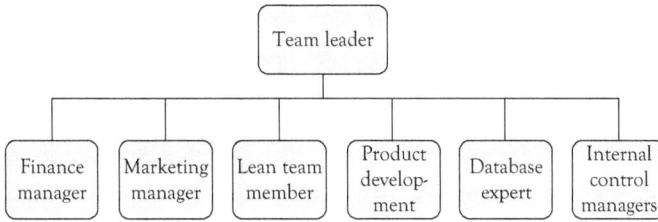

Figure 6.1. The project team.

relied on Excel, there is an argument to be made that the data should be put into a relational database so that it can be queried in a number of ways by management.

Notice that the project team also includes a member of the lean or process management team. These individuals have broad-based knowledge of the organization and can help identify activities and process structures, easing the implementation task faced by the team. And, where possible, the internal control group should be included as they often have good rapport with the rest of the organization when it comes to data collection for new information systems.

These members should, if possible, be assigned full time to the project team to speed up the initial collection and analysis of the data. While this is not always possible, the team should at least have the project as a priority among their list of assigned projects. With a full team in place, the VCMS implementation can proceed very quickly, with the team splitting up data collection tasks and improving the overall reception of the system by the workforce. Since speed of implementation is often considered one signal of a new system's viability for long-term use, it is critical that the project team have the flexibility to conduct interviews when the affected managers are available.

Once chosen, the team has to be trained to understand the difference between an activity and a task so they can help the managers in the areas they are assigned to develop a reasonable activity analysis that can be maintained with minimal effort moving forward. As we'll see, limiting the number of activities a manager can state his or her group undertakes is a vital part of creating a sustainable VCMS system. Remember, the task level data is implicitly collected when asking the managers to perform the value-add and attribute analysis.

Getting the Customer Information

The customer's preferences lie at the heart of the VCMS. That's why it is important to place a priority on collecting customer data as soon as possible in the implementation sequence. There are several steps involved in collecting this data:

1. Understanding of customer value usually comes from primary research that may include surveys to collect data on value attributes. These data can also come from secondary sources, such as interviews with sales associates or customer focus groups. Depending on the available customer value information in firms, the implementation cycle of the VCMS may be shortened if customer value data is available in a compatible format.

2. Identifying the various product or service attributes and their importance in the purchase decision is the next step in the VCMS process. There are several statistical techniques that can be used in this process. Conjoint analysis is sometimes used to determine which bundle of features/attributes is most important for customer choices and the impact of each feature on the overall purchase.[2] Sometimes statistical techniques are used, which compute implicit or hedonic prices that provide valuation of each feature out of a dollar spent. When resources are limited these data and valuation of attributes can be proxied by using customer focus groups to collect data. No matter what technique is used, it is important that data is collected from customer in the relevant market of analysis and for all relevant customer segments.

3. The project team, along with representatives from marketing, strategy, and development, should analyze all the data, identifying potential differences in attribute valuations within and across segments.

Clearly, the last step in the collection of this data requires interpretation and judgment. That is why it is important that sales and marketing who most directly interact with customers be involved in data interpretation and assessment of value attributes and their importance in each segment.

Once the customer data has been collected, attention can turn to the organization as it seeks to identify the activities that are done in the firm to meet customer value expectations. This analysis starts by gaining a clear understanding of the concept of an activity—knowing how to separate it from tasks and get it defined at a useful level.

Focusing on the "Right" Level

There truly is a right level of activity analysis in the VCMS. The key is to understand that an activity has an outcome, while tasks do not. Activities cover a broad range of tasks and can be completed by several people. In conducting the data collection for the initial launch of the VCMS, it's imperative that the managers interviewed recognize that if something they consider an activity takes less than 5% of one individual's time, it is closer to a task and should not be included.

The second question when talking about the "right" level is who should be interviewed. The research to date suggests that operating managers are at the right level of organization in terms of their knowledge and responsibility. If individuals in the department are queried, the team is more likely to end up with task data than activity data. Managers have a comprehensive view on what their group does on a daily and monthly basis and are less likely to get side-tracked by a random event that consumed significant time—they can pinpoint exceptions to the daily workflow.

Operating managers control a cost or profit center in the organization and have specific outputs assigned to them. Most operational managers have between 3 and 20 direct reports who actually do the work of the department. In a process-driven organization, the right individual to tap for data collection would be the process manager. In most organizations, it will be a department head. Identifying managers who are at the right level is critical to getting the right focus in the activity analysis and to creating a sustainable reporting system. The individual should be one level above hands-on completion of daily tasks and be responsible for the output of an area. Line managers are the optimal candidate.

Approximately Right—Avoiding the Weeds

It was suggested above that the goal is to get activities that are broad enough that the VCMS can operate and be updated with minimal effort.

There is also another reason to "avoid the weeds" in data collection, though. Once again returning to the fact that any new information system operates as a control tool inside an organization, bringing the analysis down to the task level can lead to a wide variety of potential dysfunctional consequences.

Employees can't be left with the feeling that the information they provide is going to be used against them in the future. If they have this perception, they will game the system and fail to provide useful answers. This is especially true with the willingness to state that there is waste in the daily activities performed by the subunit. In implementing the VCMS in a broad range of organizations, including service companies, the hardest thing to get managers to admit to is if there is any wasted effort in their organization. Yet, the lean management movement has repeatedly proven that there is waste in every process and every activity.

As managers answer the question about activities, it is often difficult for them to accept the fact that being approximately right is adequate for the VCMS analysis. Contrary to lean management, the goal is not to precisely define and refocus a process or activity, it is to get a general feeling as to how much of an organization's time and effort actually go to meeting customer expectations. The most valuable piece of information collected, then, is the value-added time, which is verified by having to assign that value-added activity to some element of the company's value proposition. While it may be difficult to get people to admit to waste, when they are faced with the value proposition it becomes easier to identify the degree to which their subunit really adds to the value proposition of the firm. This has been found to be the case, with managers (reluctantly, at times) reassigning their activities to one of the BVA categories.

The team can recommend a level of waste to be used for each activity, but the issue shouldn't be forced in the first pass of data collection. As the VCMS is implemented and managers see that no negative impact on their group occurs, they will increasingly take more interest and better ownership of their reporting. If the implementation can be linked to other continuous improvement efforts, it becomes easier to get managers to admit that there are improvements that can be made in every corner of the organization.

The message being delivered here is simple—the team has to ensure that the data collected is not overly detailed. Staying out of the weeds means that managers will not feel as threatened that their daily work is being queried. They quickly understand that the goal of the VCMS is to gain a strategic perspective on the organization, one that can help identify areas where customers are under- or over-served, but not to punish individuals if they are tasked with work that is administrative in nature or even wrought with waste. Keeping out of the weeds starts with a solid data collection instrument.

The Data Collection Instrument

The data collection instrument has been presented in various exhibits throughout the first five chapters of this book. What we want to do now is to step through each element of the data collection worksheet and identify the kind of information that is being collected and how to build in self-help features to make the collection of information go more smoothly for the respondents to the study.

The first phase of the analysis, and probably the most critical overall, is the identification of activities and the assignment of resources to them. As can be seen in Figure 6.2, the top portion of the spreadsheet focuses on assigning people time to the various activities being completed. Notice that the total headcount is 26 people on a daily basis in this example. They are customer service agents for Easy Air. Clearly, the operation is staffed seven days a week, potentially creating a difference between total people in the department and the average number that work per day.

Looking at the data collection sheet, there are several things that make the data collection easier for the managers. First, we note the activities that are completed by reservation specialists at Easy Air. These include booking reservations, selling tickets, accepting bags, and related activities that make sense to anyone who has interacted with the airline industry. In this example the total activities performed number 12, a good number for a department.

The next aspect the manager notes is the number of people doing each activity, such as booking reservations—20 people, 20% of their time, or the equivalent in whole people of 4. This is critical information as it

Easy air				
Activity data collection sheet				
NAME _____			Cost Center: _____	
PHONE _____			# of FTE's: 26	
FUNCTION _____				
1. Activity data matrix				
Please identify key activities performed by this cost center, the number of employees engaged in this effort, and the percentage of their time (on average) dedicated to completing the activity.				
Activity description	Number of people doing activity	% Of their time spent on activity	"People" equiv. time	Cumulative people time
Book reservations	20	20%	4	4
Sell tickets	20	25%	5	9
Accept bags	20	40%	8	17
Answer questions	20	15%	3	20
Re-route passengers	6	10%	0.6	20.6
Check-in passengers/Issue boarding pass	6	50%	3	23.6
Sell tickets at gate	6	5%	0.3	23.9
Accept bags at gate	6	5%	0.3	24.2
Information announcements	6	10%	0.6	24.8
Audit ticket list	6	10%	0.6	25.4
Ensure positive bag match	6	10%	0.6	26
Reconcile lists				
Totals	N/A	N/A	26	
			True	

Figure 6.2. Activity analysis.

pushes the cost analysis. Making the assumption that there is an average salary for reservation specialists, we can now generate a cost for each activity. What is important to note on the bottom of the people equivalent time is that the column says "True." The spreadsheet has been designed to cumulate employee time until it balances with the pivot number—in this case 26 people per day. When all of their time has been accounted for, this signal will shift from "False" to "True," helping the manager account for all of the time available in his or her department easily.

Building in these types of checks into the instrument makes it much simpler for the managers responding to the study to account for all of their department's time. Given they are making approximations of time for a group of people, they need help in ensuring that the total adds up to 100% of the available time. Building this spreadsheet is a simple task, and it makes it easier for the respondents, a key to making the project seem less onerous for the participating managers. Collecting the activity analysis data usually takes the greater part of the time required in completing the data collection analysis. Managers should be given time to "play" with the numbers until they feel that the activity analysis is a fair representation of the time spent on each major activity within the department. If you note, our sample instrument only allows for a total of 21 activities. In our work we found that by structuring the instrument this way we focus data collection on most important activities and usually succeeded in preventing the data collection process from wading into the weeds.

Having completed the activity analysis, and assuming no process analysis is being used at the same time, attention turns to assigning the activities across the value-add, business value-add, and waste categories, as seen in Figure 6.3. The total has to equal 100% for each of the activities noted. In this specific example the department surveyed works with the customers on a daily basis, therefore we expect to find that most activities performed would consist of some percentage of customer value-add. We also see, though, that this percentage can vary significantly from activity to activity.

This manager noted that 50% of the time spent rerouting passengers and selling them tickets at the gate was waste. This means the activity was not something the customer would want, and no one in the company benefitted from the activity. As noted earlier, getting to this level of clarity in the data collection might be unusual, but it should remain a goal in the data collection process.

This step in the data collection is relatively easy to complete. The biggest challenge is that managers tend to place more of their activities in the

2. Activity-value assignment

For each activity from step (1), please estimate the percentage of this effort that would be considered customer value-add (a customer would pay for it), business value-add (C, F or A), or non value-add.

Activity description	% Customer value-add	% Business value-add: current	% Business value-add: future	% Business value-add: admin.	% Non value-add	Total (must equal 100%)
Book reservations	40%	30%		20%	10%	100%
Sell tickets	30%	30%		10%	30%	100%
Accept bags	50%	30%		10%	10%	100%
Answer questions	60%	10%	10%	10%	10%	100%
Re-route passengers		30%		20%	50%	100%
Check-in passengers/Issue boarding pass	40%	30%		20%	10%	100%
Sell tickets at gate	50%	20%		20%	10%	100%
Accept bags at gate	30%	40%			30%	100%
Information announcements	20%	40%		20%	20%	100%
Audit ticket list		60%		20%	20%	100%
Ensure positive bag match		60%		20%	20%	100%
Reconcile lists		40%		40%	20%	100%

Figure 6.3. Activity to value class.

value-added category than into other categories. This leads us to the next section of the data collection process (see Figure 6.4).

As is often the case in the field-based data collection, this is the step where the "rubber meets the road." If a manager has tried to claim something is value-added that is not, they can't find an attribute to attach it to. Note how this section of the data collection is organized. If a manager has noted that an activity has any percentage of value-add, it immediately maps to this sheet using basic Excel logic. Specifically, the sheet only maps value-added activities into this section. For this manager, only the activity "Audit the ticket list" was identified as having no value-add to customers. It maps as "N/A" to this section.

Having moved over only those activities that the manager has felt have some value-added in them, the value-added component of the activity is now spread out across the value attributes that have been collected during the customer survey part of the study. Once again, the instrument has to add to 100%, making it easy for the manager to keep track of the spread of value to attributes. Building in these easy check points makes the data collection process simpler for the respondents, a fact that eases the implementation.

Having completed the activity data, resource usage, value-add component, and attribute data collection, we next transform this information into cost data that can be used in further analysis. The instrument that is used for this part of the VCMS process is presented in Figure 6.5. While this part of the instrument may look complex, it automatically fills once the budget amount is inserted and links to the data that has been collected earlier. For instance, the costs by activity are driven by the original activity analysis and the percentage of people time (equivalents) that were identified in Phase one of the data collection activity. We have frozen the total people count so the assignment of people equivalent ends up as a percentage and multiplied this times the total budget figure.

This calculation is done for all of the activities, resulting in the activity data that normally comes from an activity-based analysis exercise. Given everything has been forced to 100%, the match is simple and the results logical. The participating managers receive the immediate benefit of seeing a costed worksheet.

3. Activity to Value Attribute Weighting

For each activity you noted to be value-adding, please assign the percentage of that value that corresponds to one or more of the value attributes.

Value-adding activity	Frequency	Schedule convenience	On-time performance	Price (table stakes)	Safety record	Service quality	Ease of check-in	Ease of making reserv'ns	Frequent traveler rewards	Convenient airports	Assigned seating	Meal service	Total (must be 100%)
Book reservations				30%		30%		40%					100%
Sell tickets		20%		30%		50%							100%
Accept bags				30%		40%	30%						100%
Answer questions				40%		60%							100%
N/A													0%
Check-in passengers/Issue boarding pass				30%		20%	20%				30%		100%
Sell tickets at gate				30%		30%		40%					100%
Accept bags at gate				40%		40%	20%						100%
Information announcements				70%		30%							100%

Figure 6.4. Value-add to attributes.

Activity cost estimates

| | | | Cost Center: | | | | |

# of FTE's: 26

NAME _____

PHONE _____

FUNCTION _____

Calculation Section	Budget	$ 552,000					
Activity Description	Activity Costs	$'s Cust. Value-Add	$ BVA-C	$ BVA-F	$ BVA-A	$ NVA	Check 1
Book reservations	$84,923	$33,969	$25,477	$–	$16,985	$8,492	$84,923
Sell tickets	$106,154	$31,846	$31,846	$–	$10,615	$31,846	$106,154
Accept bags	$169,846	$84,923	$50,954	$–	$16,985	$16,985	$169,846
Answer questions	$63,692	$38,215	$6,369	$6,369	$6,369	$6,369	$63,692
Check-in passengers/Issue boarding pass	$12,738	$–	$3,822	$–	$2,548	$6,369	$12,738
Sell tickets at gate	$63,692	$25,477	$19,108	$–	$12,738	$6,369	$63,692
Accept bags at gate	$6,369	$3,185	$1,274	$–	$1,274	$637	$6,369
Information announcements	$6,369	$1,911	$2,548	$–	$–	$1,911	$6,369
Audit ticket list	$12,738	$2,548	$5,095	$–	$2,548	$2,548	$12,738
Ensure positive bag match	$12,738	$–	$7,643	$–	$2,548	$2,548	$12,738
Reconcile lists	$12,738	$–	$7,643	$–	$2,548	$2,548	$12,738
	$552,000	$222,074	$161,778	$6,369	$75,157	$86,622	$552,000

Figure 6.5. Cost to activities and attributes (continued).

	Frequency	Schedule conven- ience	On-time performance	Price (table stakes)	Safety record	Service quality	Ease of check-in	Ease of making reserv'ns	Frequent traveler rewards	Conven- ient airports	Assigned seating	Meal service	Check 2
Book reservations	$–	$–	$–	$10,191	$–	$10,191	$–	$13,588	$–	$–	$–	$–	$33,969
Sell tickets	$–	$6,369	$–	$9,554	$–	$15,923	$–		$–	$–	$–	$–	$31,846
Accept bags	$–	$–	$–	$25,477	$–	$33,969	$25,477	$–	$–	$–	$–	$–	$84,923
Answer questions	$–	$–	$–	$15,286	$–	$22,929	$–	$–	$–	$–	$–	$–	$38,215
Check-in passengers/Issue boarding pass	$–	$–	$–	$–	$–		$–	$–	$–	$–	$–	$–	$–
Sell tickets at gate	$–	$–	$–	$7,643	$–	$5,095	$5,095		$–	$–	$7,643	$–	$25,477
Accept bags at gate	$–	$–	$–	$955	$–	$955	$–	$1,274	$–	$–	$–	$–	$3,185
Information announcements	$–	$–	$–	$764	$–	$764	$382	$–	$–	$–	$–	$–	$1,911
Audit ticket list	$–	$–	$–	$1,783	$–	$764	$–	$–	$–	$–	$–	$–	$2,548
Ensure positive bag match	$–	$–	$–	$–	$–	$–	$–	$–	$–	$–	$–	$–	$–
Reconcile lists	$–	$–	$–	$–	$–	$–	$–	$–	$–	$–	$–	$–	$–
	$–	$6,369	$–	$71,654	$–	$90,592	$30,954	$14,862	$–	$–	$7,643	$–	$222,074

Figure 6.5. Cost to activities and attributes (continued).

The spread to value-added versus business value-add and waste is done by linking the information in the second section of the worksheet to the corresponding columns in the costing analysis. Here we are taking the activity cost and spreading it based on the information provided. Finally, the section on value attributes is "blown out." Once again, a simple Excel command linking from the value-added dollars through the value attribute weightings is used to develop the cost analysis.

Hopefully walking through the data collection instrument has made it clear that VCMS implementation can be done in a straightforward fashion. We often notice that firms don't consume the fixed assets, or operating costs in the same way as the people time. In this case, a column is added to the cost analysis section of the data sheet that allows the respondent to add these additional operating costs to those activities that benefit from them. In our experience we have seldom needed to make this adjustment.

Automation—Key to Success

What the preceding section has shown is that automation is the key to success in collecting data, whether it is for the VCMS or a more simplified process or activity analysis. Linking accounting to the operations of the firm has one basic requirement: the data collected has to add to 100% on all key dimensions. With this information in place, and a budget to work from (*Note*: budgets were used, not accounting ledger data), the completion of the data collection phase can proceed quite rapidly.

At Easy Air, managers were brought in waves to a room that had a bank of computers. The data collection instrument was introduced to the managers in a short and focused presentation, and then the facilitators moved around the room helping individuals who had perhaps inadvertently wiped out a cell formula or were having other difficulties. The advantage to this approach is sustainability. Once managers have filled in the worksheet one time on their own, providing subsequent data becomes much more straightforward. The key to success is the automation of as much of the data analysis as is possible.

The results of the Excel analysis can be directly incorporated in an Access database as long as the underlying data sheets are never compromised. While the research team relied upon Excel to do the follow-up analysis, there is no reason why a database expert couldn't transform the data collected into a relational database that would make subsequent analysis simpler. The more automated the process, the easier it is to complete, and the more likely the resulting information can become a permanent part of the company's archive of strategically oriented customer data.

Summary

This chapter has laid out the first phase in implementing the VCMS approach in an organization—setting up the implementation team and gathering the dataset. Starting with identifying a strong change champion, one who has influence in both the marketing and finance functional areas as a starting requirement, attention turns to creating a cross-functional team that can move across the organization collecting the data that lies at the heart of the system.

The actual data collection is a streamlined exercise when using a consistent instrument. The critical step in the process is identifying the activities at the appropriate level and in the right number. It would be easy to get caught up in the weeds, going too deep in the analysis. Using operational managers often helps alleviate this potential challenge, as does structuring the instrument by putting in cut-offs for the total number of activities that can be used as well as minimums for the amount of employee time consumed by an activity. Taking time to get the activities properly defined is critical for getting data that is useful for the purpose of VCMS. Once activities have been defined, they are sorted and apportioned in value-add, business value-add, and waste categories. The proof of the pudding for value-add comes when the manager is required to spread the value-added activity across the customer-defined value attributes. If the activity doesn't match or connect to one of the attributes, it is not value-add.

Using data analysis programs, the addition of the department's budget number is all that is needed to complete the worksheet. When the data collection instrument connects the attribute and the cost information, managers understand how and if the resources in their departments are used to deliver value. The first phase of the VCMS results in a series of spreadsheets that contain an extended activity analysis.

If the firm wants to implement activity-based costing at this stage, it simply needs to add drivers to the activity data. If activity-based budgeting is wanted, little has to be done except to ensure the data collection is done on an ongoing basis, with control system checks put in place to ensure that the money is spent where intended. The VCMS, then, provides data that can be used in multiple ways within the organization and fits within the profile of many of the modern management tools in terms of data requirements. What it adds to the picture are the value attributes, the linkage to the customer that is vital for long-term growth.

> *It seems necessary to completely shed the old skin before the new, brighter,*
> *stronger, and more beautiful one can emerge ... I never thought I'd be getting a life lesson from a snake.*
>
> Julie Ridge[3]

CHAPTER 7

Implementing a Value-Based Cost Management System— Part II: Collecting and Analyzing the Data

Money is like water. When water is moving and flowing, it cleanses, it purifies, it makes things green, it's beautiful. But when it starts to slow down and sludge, it becomes toxic and stagnant.

Lynne Twist[1]

At the heart of the value-based cost management system (VCMS) lies the simple fact that money is the lifeblood of the organization. The goal of the VCMS is to ensure that this money flows in the direction valued by customers. Creating a constant cycle of invest-harvest-reinvest, the VCMS is an engine of growth that helps unite the organization in its quest for creating superior value for the customers who determine the ultimate worth of the company's endeavors. Because it is a top-line-driven growth model, the VCMS requires education to ensure that the benefits are reaped and the data collected is reliable. The VCMS process begins with education of key stakeholders and communication with the firm's employees to build awareness and knowledge of the VCMS and to help them understand the goals of the VCMS.

Education—A Major Step

Educating the managers of the organization on the goals and structure of the VCMS is a critical and essential major step in the VCMS implementation. This education can be done through a series of meetings offered at various times to assure maximum possible attendance. These meetings provide an opportunity to air concerns and to ensure that there is a sound understanding of the project, its goals, and what will be required from each manager and each work group. In our experience we have learned that when the CEO leads the first meeting, this has a positive impact on the success of the project and a strong influence on the firm's managers and their acceptance of the project.

Our field work experience has shown that it is best to start the initial meeting with managers by sharing with them a specific example and results from the electronics firm field work presented in Chapter 2. The second major model that has proven useful to explain the concepts underlying the implementation is the VCMS "target" diagram. This introduction places the VCMS project in the right context—a quest to do a better job serving the final customer. It is also important to lay out the customer value profile during this meeting, so managers clearly understand that the model is customer-driven. What issues should be addressed during this meeting?

- The fact that the model is customer-driven should be emphasized.
- Customer value profile data should be presented.
- Clear definitions of value-add, business value-add, and waste should be developed.
- The data collection requirements should be discussed.
- An example of how the data is collected should be walked through.
- Specific mention of the strategic nature of the project should be made.
- Reinforcement of the fact that the project is not concerned with operational control should take place.
- Any linkages to other continuous improvement initiatives, either currently underway or recently completed, should be stressed.
- If process data is to be collected, the process framework should be presented.
- The way the data is to be used should be emphasized.

- The importance of being willing to identify waste in the activity analysis needs to be stressed as the basis for improving performance by redirecting these resources to value-added work.

Ample time needs to be left for questions, as managers are often interested in knowing whether this is a one-time study or a long-term implementation and frequently have many questions about the bullet diagram. Since the data will need to be collected and then updated on a regular basis, it is important that time is provided to make managers comfortable with the data collection instrument and its targeted usage so that they can manage this instrument on their own after the initial data collection is completed.

When the meetings are over, managers should be queried via e-mail to determine if they have any further questions or concerns. This e-mail should also collect information for scheduling the project interview so that the interview team can begin to develop a work plan. It may take follow-up e-mails and phone calls to get all of the managers scheduled. This is one of the major tasks performed by the interview team. It needs to be managed efficiently to ensure that interviews are held to the 30- to 45-minute time allotment that has been found to be needed to complete the data collection interview. If managers have been effectively briefed during the first educational meeting, the interview team's job is made much simpler and the task can be shortened significantly. It is recommended that the team allows one hour in their schedules to complete each interview because they may end up with questions of their own or need to spend time reviewing the results.

The Interview Team

The section above notes the fact that there is an interview team. This is a subset of the total team that is dedicated to the project on a full time basis. Our work suggests that the interview team needs to consist of managers at roughly the same level as the managers being interviewed to prevent the feeling that management is intruding in the department's business (see Figure 7.1). If the organization has an internal control group, it is often quite useful to task these individuals as the interview team because managers

Figure 7.1. The interview team.

are more accustomed to answering questions from this group. The same holds true for employees that have been involved in the lean management initiatives. These employees have earned trust in their respective organizations and might be more effective in collecting not only information about value add but also information about activities that might be wasteful.

Since the interview team bears the brunt of the data collection, each member should be fully trained on the structure of the data collection instrument. The team members need to be comfortable with the instrument and be able to correct specific calculations if the data instrument becomes compromised during the interview process. The composition of the data collection team, then, needs to include mid-level managers who are respected for their discretion and honesty in the organization. Highly political individuals do not work out well, as their motives can be questioned, leading to false responses by the interviewees or noncompliance with the project in general. Clearly there is no avoiding politics, but the project should aim to be as apolitical as possible in order to be as successful as possible in reaching its objectives.

Completing the Data Collection Instrument

Chapter 6 walked through the various segments of the data collection instrument. The data collection starts by filling in the basic information about the respondent—name, department, and contact number. The next question is the number of full-time equivalent employees that work for the department. While this seems like a straightforward question, the presence of part-time workers, shared workers, and in Easy Air's case seven days of operation can make this question difficult to answer. Since this number drives a majority of the key calculations, it's important that this number makes sense to the manager. At Easy Air the decision was made to use staffing on an average day. The department had more people than the daily total because they had to cover seven days of operation. But the data collected focused on an average day of work, so daily numbers were used throughout.

Once the number of individuals, namely full-time equivalents, is agreed upon, attention turns to noting what activities are done by the department. The manager needs to have a sound understanding of the key activities his or her group is expected to complete. Some managers prefer to develop the entire list of activities first, and then go back and assign people time to them. Others work one activity at a time, completing all of the data input for each activity as they go. The team member should accede to the preferences of the responding manager to make the data collection more comfortable for the manager.

It takes the most time to collect the activity data and then assign people time to the various activities. The manager needs to identify how many people are involved in each activity and on average what percentage of these individual's time is allocated to the activity. If not all employees spend the same amount of time on the activity, then an average needs to be calculated. The team member should carry a simple 10-key calculator for cases such as this.

The sheet automatically tallies the total time being assigned, resulting in a shift from "false" to "true" at the bottom of the section when all of the people time has been accounted for. Getting to "true" often requires several iterations, with the potential of having to "force" one activity's time to get the total accounted for properly—100% is critical for the accounting aspect of the analysis. Once this step is completed, attention can turn to the value-add and attribute data.

The assignment of value-add is done across the five categories (value-add, business value-add—indirect, business value-add—future, business value-add—administrative, and waste), totaling to 100%. The worksheet shows this total, so it usually only takes a few minutes to complete this section. It is vital for the team member to stress that there is waste in every activity. The responding manager may still hold back in assigning waste to the department's activities, but the attempt needs to be made to have at least some level of waste noted. This is where it's important to explain that there's no room for improvement if there isn't any waste to be removed.

Only those activities that are designated as having customer value-add map to the next section of the data collection instrument. Now attention turns to assigning the activity's value to one of the predetermined attributes. In our field work we have found that managers often find this challenging, especially if they included activities as value-add that really aren't value-adding in the customer's eyes. This step presents an opportunity to bring the customer value perspective into the organization and share with managers the key data gathered during the customer data collection phase. The attribute data collected needs to sum to 100%. The instrument should automatically keep track of this amount.

The team members need to know the amount of total budget by department. In practice we often observed that if the team member has this information in advance, then a good way to start the meeting is by the manager and team member agreeing that they are both working with the same budget for the department. If an error exists in the budget summary sheet from finance, then the error can get cleared early in the process. In case of discrepancy, the team member needs to use the manager's estimate, leaving reconciliation with finance as a follow-on task. The number is placed in the preset "budget" box on the lower portion of the instrument. The entire financial picture then automatically fills in, a result which usually pleases the participating manager.

Once the interview is completed and all the data is collected, it is best to share a copy immediately with the responding manager. This step is critical for the visibility of the project—managers have to feel that they own their data and have control over it. In our field work, we've experienced occasions where a manager wanted to make changes to the data sheet after the interview. We recommend that this be allowed, as filling out the sheet the first time is a learning experience.

Creating a Master File

All of the managers do not have to be interviewed before the data for all departments is organized in the master file. In this part of the process, the database experts can be very useful. Depending on how the information is going to be used, it may be appropriate to transfer all of the data into a relational database, such as an Access database. Because this is one option for creating the master file, it is critical that every worksheet completed by the interview team be identical. No matter what software is used, it's still critical that all the worksheets used for data collection remain the same so the analysis and compilation can go smoothly and without additional adjustments or interpretations.

If process data has been collected during the data collection phase, the master file should be sorted by process codes (see Chapter 8 for more details) and summarized. This often presents a learning experience for the company, as the cross-functional nature of the activities that make up the process becomes visible. One of the activities in the process that in our experience receives the greatest amount of time and money in most VCMS studies is management itself. The size of this number often leads to immediate suggestions in a company to cut back on the reporting and meetings requirements for their managers so more time can go to value-adding work. Since management is mostly an administrative task, it seldom results in customer value-add. If an organization is spending inordinate amounts of money simply managing itself, it will find it harder to compete in the global marketplace compared to organizations with a leaner management structure.

The master data file should retain the department information for each activity reported. This information usually needs to be added to the data collection worksheet and can become a column that automatically fills with the departments' abbreviated name or number. It is data that has usually been added as the master file was put together, but there is no reason why it can't become part of the master data collection sheet. It just requires a new column and a new pivot cell where the data is entered.

The master data file needs to focus on the bottom segment of the worksheet, where the activities and value attributes have been assigned a monetary value. The top part of the worksheet is to ease data collection—the key analysis using the data will focus on the financial aspects of the organization's operations. A master folder of all the completed worksheets should be kept so that future data collection is made more efficient, but the master file itself emphasizes the financial analysis contained in the datasheets.

The Informative Cost Summary

Once all of the departments' data have been collected and a master file of the financial results compiled, attention turns to actually creating the informative cost summary. For this purpose the dollars of value-add, business value-add, and waste are summarized, as is the total dollar amount applied to each value attribute. This analysis needs to be summarized for the organization as a whole. Since the dollars of value-add by value attribute are crucial for the development of the multipliers, this information is a critical output of the informative cost summary.

The results of this analysis make up the first part of the management report. It allows management to see whether, in general, the resources of the firm are being directed toward the activities and outcomes prioritized by the management. When spending on business value-add—future activities is low in the organization, this is clearly visible. In our field work, waste is usually somewhere around 20% in most organizations, although getting managers to identify this level of waste in the early stages of the VCMS implementation is often challenging. If waste is greater than 20%, it signals that the company might need to undertake a lean initiative if it isn't already doing so.

Value-add should also be somewhere in the 20% range as a benchmark. In firm after firm studied to develop the VCMS, value-add has been very close to 20%. Given that this data is the key to understanding whether a company is pursuing customer requirements in a profitable way, if it is below 20% the firm will likely be struggling with profitability. If the sum is greater than 20%, the firm might be highly customer-focused or operating in a differentiated market and is therefore more likely to have higher profitability.

If customer segment data has been developed (see Figure 7.2), it is important to add this feature to the data collection sheet. This usually requires the insertion of another section that queries how much of an activity goes to a specific customer segment. Once again tallying to 100%, this data is straightforward to collect. It results, though, in two summaries in the financial analysis—one for the company as a whole and one by segment. This is when using a relational database becomes useful, as it becomes fairly complex to maintain all of these data in Excel. If the

2. Customer segment information						
Process code	Activity	Business traveler	Leisure traveler	Seniors	None	Total
10.3.2	Provide internal financial information				100%	100%
13.1.1	Creating measurement systems	25%	25%	25%	25%	100%
13.1.4	Measuring cost	40%	30%	30%		100%
13.1.6	Measuring productivity	20%	20%	20%	40%	100%
13.3.2	Conducting process benchmarking	25%	25%	25%	25%	100%
13.3.3	Conducting competitve benchmarking	40%	40%	20%		100%
13.4.2	Implementing continuous process improvement				100%	100%
13.4.3	Reengineering business processes and systems				100%	100%
13.4.4	Managing transition to change	20%	20%	20%	40%	100%
6.1.1	Select and certify suppliers				100%	100%
13.4.2	Implement continuous process improvement				100%	100%
5.5.3.4	Managing MRO service providers				100%	100%
10.1.1	Budgeting				100%	100%
8.6.5	Meetings	15%	20%	15%	50%	100%
8.4.4	Training	20%	20%	20%	40%	100%
6.3.2.14	Downtime				100%	100%
8.5.3	Supervision/mentoring				100%	100%
8.5.3	Managing team performance	20%	20%	20%	40%	100%

Figure 7.2. Customer segment data.

company treats all customers alike (a generic strategy), customer segment information does not need to be collected. A process-oriented result for Windows, Inc. is presented in Figure 7.3. The results are for the first process—the development of a strategy.

Developing and Interpreting Value Multipliers

Having traced the resource consumption of the firm to specific value attributes, it is now possible to combine the revenue equivalents by value attribute with the value-added cost for that attribute. As you may remember, the value multiplier is calculated by dividing the revenue equivalent by the value-added dollars that are needed to deliver that value attribute. If the company doesn't pursue a market segmentation strategy, there will be only one set of multipliers. If segments are managed differently, though, then two sets of multipliers will be developed—one for the company in general and one that details results by segment. Finally, if the data collection suggests that there is more than one segment, as was found at Impact, Inc., then multipliers may be needed for each newly identified segment.

An example of the value multipliers by segment for General Telecom (GTI), one of the earliest projects completed in the VCMS analysis is presented in Figure 7.4. The goal is to present the data in such a way that management can have a strategic perspective where they are spending too much or too little to deliver on specific components of the value profile. This is a critical part of the data analysis that needs to be shared with management.

Looking at the value multipliers for GTI, we observe that the average multipliers are below 5 except for the local service customers, who were relatively happy with the company's service. The company was perceived as responsive to traditional customers and had convenient bill paying locations, suggesting that the high multipliers on these attributes were competitive strengths. Unfortunately, the local service customers weren't valued by the firm as they were perceived as being satisfied with a dial tone only. GTI's managers were actively pursuing the Internet segment, where our analysis shows that most of its spending was wasted (multipliers of zero). In this segment GTI had a high rating on speed

Distribution of activity costs by cost category	$'S customer value-add	$'S business value-add: current	$'S business value-add: future	$'S business value-add: admin.	$'S non value-add	Distribution of value-added costs by value attribute							
						Price (e.g., basic product)	Options (color / grilles)	Appearance	Brand	Warranty/ durability	Sizes avail- able	Respon- sive- ness of company	Quality of service
	$–	$55,888	$6,210	$–	$–	$–	$–	$–	$–	$–	$–	$–	$–
	$–	$26,501	$92,755	$145,758	$–	$–	$–	$–	$–	$–	$–	$–	$–
	$5,801	$9,281	$5,801	$2,320	$–	$1,740	$–	$1,740	$–	$1,740	$–	$–	$580
	$–	$–	$598,547	$–	$–	$–	$–	$–	$–	$–	$–	$–	$–
	$–	$141,824	$159,552	$35,456	$17,728	$–	$–	$–	$–	$–	$–	$–	$–
	$5,801	$233,495	$862,864	$183,534	$17,728	$1,740	$–	$1,740	$–	$1,740	$–	$–	$580

Figure 7.3. Tracing costs to attributes.

Summary of customer multiplier by segment			
Revenue equivalent			
Value attribute	Long distance customers	Internet customers	Local service customers
Price of service	$87,100.00	$11,400.00	$56,650.00
Speed/ease of access	$–	$19,000.00	$–
Responsiveness	$43,550.00	$–	$226,600.00
Convenient locations	$21,775.00	$–	$113,300.00
Easy to understand bills	$32,662.50	$–	$56,650.00
Variety of services available	$32,662.50	$7,600.00	$113,300.00
Total	$217,750.00	$38,000.00	$566,500.00
Value add $'s (in thousands)	$50,610.7	$10,260.0	$100,553.8
Value add $'s per attribute			
Price of service	$15,183.21	$2,590.91	$29,815.79
Speed/ease of access	$–	$1,544.72	$–
Responsiveness	$7,640.35	$–	$15,106.67
Convenient locations	$2,531.98	$–	$5,035.56
Easy to understand bills	$5,025.00	$–	$8,583.33
Variety of services available	$15,183.21	$–	$29,815.79
Total	$50,610.70	$10,260.00	$100,553.80
Value multiplier by segment			
Price of service	5.7	4.4	1.9
Speed/ease of access	0.0	12.3	0.0
Responsiveness	5.7	0.0	15.0
Convenient locations	8.6	0.0	22.5
Easy to understand bills	6.5	0.0	6.6
Variety of services available	2.2	1.6	3.8
Average multiplier	4.3	3.7	5.6

Figure 7.4. Value multipliers by segment.

and ease of access, suggesting it was doing a good job for this segment, but our analysis shows that the other two segments didn't value this spending at all. This was significant and valuable information for GTI's management team.

The VCMS system clearly shows the value of customer segment data to aid the firm in evaluating its strategy. After the field work was completed at GTI, more attention was paid to the local customer, who was identified as the cash cow for the company. Spending on the Internet segment was disciplined so that the activities that were valued by the Internet customer segment received the greatest attention while spending was cut back on other attributes not valued as strongly by this segment. Finally, effort was reduced in terms of providing options to long-distance customers as this low multiplier suggested the firm was overspending on this activity.

The value multipliers are the ultimate objective of the VCMS system. They provide the strategic evaluations so critically needed by firms seeking to maximize the value they create for customers. Finding out exactly what customers value, and by how much, can help the firm focus its internal activities into areas that provide the best pay-offs. As was determined at GTI, a one-size-fits-all operating structure could result in some very dissatisfied customers.

For the local service customer, at the time of this study, Internet access just didn't matter. This result would probably be different if the study was done again, as most homes now have Internet access and many different providers are competing on an ongoing basis for this business. This fact underscores the need to revisit the VCMS analysis and update the data regularly. If the information is used to support continuous improvement activities, the internal data needs to be collected monthly or quarterly. And, a customer-centered firm needs to be in continuous contact with its customers to learn how and if customers value specific attributes. It is also important to see if the level of competition in the market is changing and to find out how well the company is doing in meeting changing customer expectations. Once the VCMS data collection instrument has been mastered it is relatively easy to keep the data current and monitor how well the organization is doing in meeting its goals.

Reporting Back Out

Once the data analysis has been completed, it is very important to share results with the managers who were part of the project. The results of the VCMS study need to be shared with everyone in the organization who participated in the data collection process or might in some way be connected to the project. In order for the VCMS to have an organization-wide impact, everyone needs to see the results of the data collection and the final analysis.

When everyone is informed about how well, or poorly, the company is doing in meeting customer requirements, more time and attention can be paid by individual managers and departments to ensuring that spending is directed toward those activities customers value. Change initiatives that are driven by what is now a well-defined strategy are the result of a successful VCMS initiative. Communicating the strategic objectives is now given new shape and direction—the VCMS makes the strategy of the firm visible and actionable. Serving as a new communication tool that unites the entire organization in the goal of meeting and exceeding the delivery of customer value and meeting customer expectations is one of the strongest justifications for implementing the VCMS. Strategy and activities are placed within a common framework and measures are used to reinforce the goals of the customer-centered organization.

So, reporting back out means more than holding a top management briefing meeting. Clearly this needs to take place, but the results of the study need to be made part of the monthly reporting package that all managers receive. In doing so, the VCMS becomes part of the structure of the firm, keeping everyone's eyes focused on serving the customer.

Building VCMS In to the Management System

As the previous discussion suggests, it is important to build the VCMS into the management structure of the firm. Since the multipliers and value-added information provide key indicators of how successful the firm is in directing its spending and activities to those areas valued by customers, it is important that the VCMS not be a one-off study, but rather part of the daily lexicon of the organization.

There are several ways that the VCMS can be built into the management system. These include the following:

- Monthly reports by department of the value-added results.
- Monthly reports of the overall results of the company against its customer segments.

- Inclusion of the VCMS results by month in the monthly management briefings.
- Tying of the VCMS to other continuous improvement projects underway, such as lean process management.
- Linking of the VCMS to the strategic language of the firm.
- Movement to homogenize the language of the firm regarding its customers to reflect the VCMS structure.
- Building the VCMS structure into the budgeting system of the organization
- Using some aspects of improvement on the VCMS metrics as part of the formal evaluation system.

The goal is to make the VCMS part of the regular reporting routine, improving, and evaluating the performance of the organization. Strategic in nature, the VCMS provides a signal to everyone in the organization about those activities which are more likely to create customer value. It has also been found that by including business value-add indirect, employees can identify which activities touch the customer in some way. Every time a customer is put first in a decision, the company overall makes choices focused on the correct objective. Putting the customer first in every activity is the ultimate objective. It is an ongoing project, not a one-time study.

Summary

In this chapter we continued the discussion of the implementation of the VCMS, emphasizing how the data is collected by a subteam of the implementation team. Focus was also placed on how the VCMS data is analyzed, including the development of segmented data that can help the company focus its attention away from a one-size-fits-all strategy to one where the individual segment needs of the customer population are served.

The key in any implementation is good communication. When the data from the VCMS study is analyzed, its results need to be distributed among all the participating managers if the study is to achieve its ultimate objective—creating a new language for communicating the alignment of strategic objectives with operational actions. In developing a VCMS, the input of managers and individuals across the organization is needed. It is only logical that after the analysis is done these same individuals are given the results to help them refocus their group's efforts.

The VCMS, then, is an externally driven but internally sourced basis for strategic analysis and direction-giving. As we saw with GTI, the value multipliers can be very different between segments, suggesting that a firm has to be aware of how its actions are interpreted across the various customer segments rather than relying on a generic strategy for all customers. Having walked through the basic characteristics of the VCMS and how it can be used in organizations, attention is now going to turn to specific uses of the data reports that are created. The VCMS provides a basis for incremental analysis, strategic analysis, and operational analysis that can be used in a common framework to improve organizational performance. The result is one language, one set of meanings that can be used to focus attention on a myriad number of problems and situations. That is the beauty of the VCMS—elegant information, consistently delivered for use across the organization.

Some succeed because they are destined to; most succeed because they are determined to.

Anatole France[2]

CHAPTER 8

Value Creation and Process Management

To be what we are, and to become what we are capable of becoming, is the only end of life.

Spinoza[1]

In this chapter, we turn to the linkage of the value-based cost management system (VCMS) to process management, one of the major innovations being used by organizations to eliminate waste and improve responsiveness to customer requests. Using an example from the U.S. Coast Guard Academy, we trace how the VCMS data collection instrument can also be used to capture process information. We've already seen this data represented in the Easy Air data collection instrument, but now we'll spend some more time trying to understand how this data is both classified as well as how the process framework can be implemented. We'll begin with what is likely a review of process management itself and then move on to the application of the VCMS in a process framework.

The Basic Concept of Process Management

Process management is concerned with managing the horizontal flow of activities and products, emphasizing the handing off of a task or piece of paper, or project between individuals and departments.[2] The goal is to streamline this horizontal workflow, removing all forms of waste that may occur, such as rework and fumbles that occur in the white space between individuals or departments in the flow. A process, then, is the flow of activities in which people work and departments organize. That means that most processes are cross-functional in nature, knitting together the organization into a smooth flow of activities and outputs that serve the needs of the company's customers.

When companies begin to take a process perspective to their organization's workflows, attention automatically turns to identifying waste and inefficiencies in the existing processes. Disconnects in the workflow (i.e., nonvalue-added steps, redundancies, bottlenecks, and unnecessary documentation and activities) create breaks in the smooth processing of documents or products. There can also be executional disconnects, including lack of skills, inadequate computer systems, impractical policies, internal politics, incentive conflicts, and an unsupportive culture. Executional disconnects have a simple result—the company may not be the best at performing the work encapsulated by the process.

Identifying the "should" state for a process requires significant effort. Narrowing down the activities and supporting documentation to just the steps required to complete the work can leave some employees feeling that their job might be eliminated. Since the ratio of time required to complete a process as it should flow versus how it currently flows is one to five[3] (or 20% of the time is all that should be spent), there are job implications in a process redesign. If 80% of the work being done is unnecessary, it means that some people's entire workday is spent doing things to correct errors and fill process gaps. This fact makes process improvement projects very challenging but essential if a company is to gain or regain competitive excellence.

As can be seen in Figure 8.1, there are a variety of decisions that have to be made in a process workflow. Each of these decision points can cause delay in the processing of the order. This is not a perfect process workflow, but an example of one that has been documented in a company. A simple process, one where orders are filled from a warehouse, requires that the order itself be handled, going all the way to the end when payment is received from the customer. The "D"-shaped figures all represent delays in the flow that extend the time required to meet customer requests. One of the worst of these is in the initial part of the flow, when orders are batched up for weekly processing. In a well-designed flow, orders would be handled as soon as they are received.

One can easily imagine that there are other delays due to batching or insufficient workforce. If the orders didn't originate as a batch, it is likely that the credit "sidebar" could take place almost immediately upon entry of the order. If there are credit problems, though, it is logical that these

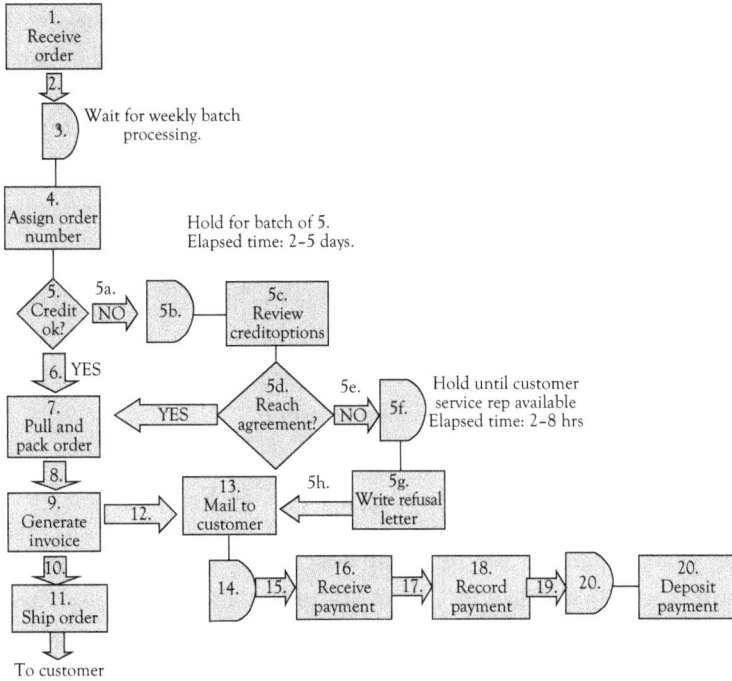

Figure 8.1. Example of a process workflow.

would delay shipment to some extent, but not the batching-based delay that occurs in this example.

In developing an "is" or current state of a process, such as in this example, the goal is to be as realistic as possible. Improvements are usually easy to spot, such as removing the delays that occur in the flow. Some side activities are unavoidable, but they should be streamlined so that the customer knows what the problem is and can quickly address it so that the order can be filled. Once all of the delays and unnecessary decision points have been removed, a "should" or ideal state diagram can be generated. Bridging the gap between the "is" and "should" process flows is the focus of improvement projects.

For instance, the process could be made electronic through the use of a website ordering system. Order entry would be automatic, with order numbers assigned by the underlying software. All of the steps involved in the credit check could be handled with a verification service, which provides almost instantaneous feedback to the customer, who can then propose a different payment approach. The order could then be picked and shipped the same day, using the shipping mode requested by the customer. Payment is automatic in this system also, so all of the waiting in that process can also be eliminated.

If the company can't convert to being completely electronic, it can at least use order entry software and credit verification software to trim time from the process flow. For example, using PayPal or credit cards can eliminate the payment delay, perhaps even generating a cost savings that can be passed on to the customer to encourage this change in behavior. All of these options have to be made available in the "should" design phase of the process. In the end, then, process management entails examining and improving the flow of work in the organization.

VCMS and Developing a Process Framework

The VCMS approach was originally designed to interface with process management approaches. By including a process code in the data attributes captured by the survey, process management implementation is supported. The process starts, though, with the development of a process framework. The standard for this type of framework is the one developed by the APQC International Benchmarking Clearinghouse.[4] This framework consists of 13 major processes, seven of which are used to provide direct service to customers and the remaining six for internal support. What are the 13 processes within this framework?

1. Understand markets and customers
2. Develop vision and strategy
3. Design products and services
4. Market and sell
5. Produce and deliver for manufacturing organizations
6. Produce and deliver for service organizations
7. Invoice and service customers
8. Develop and manage human resources
9. Manage information
10. Manage financial and physical resources
11. Execute environmental management program
12. Manage external relationships
13. Manage improvement and change

Included in the framework is second- and third-tier numbering systems that further break down each of the major processes into significant steps and activities. Serving as one of the most widely used process frameworks, the APQC Process Framework provides a way for companies to compare themselves to other firms using preset definitions and classifications of work.

In each application of the VCMS, the APQC Process Framework has been used as a starting point. Modifications have been made to make the framework fit the unique nature of an industry, such as airlines for Easy Air and education for the U.S. Coast Guard Academy (USCGA). Figure 8.2 lays out the modified framework that was developed for the USCGA. As can be seen, the direct touch processes were increased to 10 from the 7 in the APQC Framework. The support processes were also expanded and modified to fit the unique environment of an educational institution.

The direct processes had two specific "outcome" stopping points. First, the school had to find and enroll cadets that would best fit the unique culture of the USCGA and the demands this environment placed on cadets. Second, the institution had to graduate and deploy effective

Planning & tactical processes	
	1. Understand USCG requirement & expectations
	2. Develop vision & strategy for the academy
	3. Design programs and pedagogical materials
	4. Develop marketing & recruiting strategy
	5. Identify, recruit & enroll cadets
	6. Deliver academic programs
	7. Develop military knowledge
	8. Develop and ensure cadet wellness
	9. Deliver training programs (LDC)
	10. Graduate and deploy effective officers
Management & support processes	11. Manage personnel and administration activities
	12. Information resource management
	13. Manage financial and physical resources
	14. Manage legal and medical support functions
	15. Manage academic/accreditation records
	16. Execute community services programs
	17. Manage improvement and change

Figure 8.2. Process framework for the U.S. Coast Guard Academy.

officers. Both of these output processes have unique activities that are required to be completed. Some of these activities fell under other processes, but there were a long series of activities that were directly driven by both enrolling suitable cadets and graduating them to become U.S. Coast Guard (USCG) officers.

No attempt was made at the academy to take this numbering system any deeper than the major process level. Since this was a learning experience for the entire academy, it was deemed adequate to understand what the major processes consumed in terms of scarce academy resources. All of the activities that were traced to a major process could have been studied to develop a second tier of numerical coding, but since this exercise was just a small part of a much larger project, this work was not completed.

The APQC has developed frameworks for a variety of industries, as seen at www.apqc.org/process-classification-framework. The industry frameworks include aerospace, automotive, banking, education, and pharmaceuticals, just to name a few. In doing benchmarking, the process framework becomes invaluable as it ensures a company is comparing apples with apples when it queries the cost and effectiveness of other companies' processes.

Tying Activities to Processes

The VCMS uses the process framework information to provide more targeted analysis of where the firm is creating value for its customers and where it is spending its support dollars. Since all of the support functions in the standard process framework are administrative in nature, if too many respondents to the in-house survey perform administrative activities there might be a problem. Since BVA_A activities never generate revenue, but instead remove profit or scarce resources from the organization, it is important to keep tabs on how much it costs to run the organization. A good goal is to reduce these costs to between 15% and 20% of total revenue dollars. The goal is to shift excess administrative costs over to value-add or BVA_F activities.

Since the goal is to tie the activities reported during the data collection phase to specific processes or process steps, the process framework, modified to fit the organization, needs to be developed before data collection begins. Our field work shows that it is usually best to have a small cross-functional team develop this framework, one that understands how to define the levels in the framework without getting into too much detail. The activities that are collected during the study provide the detailed information, while the framework is there to help classify activities by process. An example of the application of the process framework for the USCGA study is shown in Figure 8.3.

Once the framework has been developed, an additional step is added to the data collection phase. Specifically, the respondent needs to help classify each of the activities identified against the process framework. We suggest that the team allocate approximately 45 minutes for the interview activity in a process-based VCMS study. The next question to be answered is the timing of the process data collection. Our field work indicates that it is best to complete the value-add and attribute data collection of the instrument first, and then add the process classification data to the top of the worksheet. This information will then automatically be filled into the other sections of the data collection instrument. Clearly, the more detailed the process framework is, the longer it can take during the interview process to gather the corresponding data.

Notice in Figure 8.3 that the data collection instrument has also been expanded to include the workgroup as part of the activity data tags. The reason for this is simple. When the data is summarized by process step, it's important to know where the activity takes place. This makes the development of a process team to implement process management easier because the affected parts of the organization are already identified. It is sometimes quite surprising to see what parts of an organization are involved in making a process function.

Summarizing the Data by Process

Once the data has been collected, it has to be summarized by process step. If the data is in a relational database, a simple report is created. If, on the other hand, the data is entered into a program such as Excel, the data showing the financials (the last part of the data collection instrument) has to be copied into a master data sheet. This master data sheet can then be sorted by process code. In either case, a summary report that looks something like Figure 8.4 can then be generated.

CC	Process code	Calculation section — Activity description	Budget $306,900 — Activity costs	$306,900 — % Direct student benefit	$284,900 — % Indirect support of student activities	Personnel — % Future academy value-add	$22,000 — % Acad admin	Operating — % Non value-add
gp	14	Generate transcripts	$30,690	$–	$24,552	$–	$3,069	$3,069
gp	3	Build master schedule	$45,012	$27,007	$9,002	$–	$4,501	$4,501
gp	12	Decision support–CGA	$76,725	$–	$23,018	$23,018	$15,345	$15,345
gp	11	Manage/evaluate personnel	$5,115	$–	$–	$–	$4,092	$1,023
gp	12	Register students	$5,115	$3,069	$1,023	$–	$512	$512
gp	12	Produce cadet schedules	$10,230	$6,138	$2,046	$–	$1,023	$1,023
gp	12	Add/drop activities/adjustments	$10,230	$6,138	$2,046	$–	$1,023	$1,023
gp	6	Academic reviews	$2,046	$–	$818	$–	$614	$614
gp	12	Degree audits	$5,115	$–	$–	$3,069	$1,023	$1,023
gp	12	Registration audits	$1,023	$–	$–	$614	$205	$205
gp	15	Field inquiries from depts, students, etc.	$10,230	$–	$3,069	$3,069	$2,046	$2,046
gp	14	Filing & recordkeeping	$20,460	$–	$–	$–	$16,368	$4,092
gp	2	Manage information system development	$30,690	$–	$–	$24,552	$6,138	$–
gp	11	Professional development	$10,230	$–	$–	$8,184	$–	$2,046
gp	3	Product course catalog–maintain	$30,690	$18,414	$6,138	$–	$3,069	$3,069
gp	14	Meetings/Projects–Administrative	$10,230	$–	$–	$–	$8,184	$2,046
gp	3	Meetings/Projects–Curricular	$1,023	$–	$307	$307	$205	$205
gp	2	Planning meetings/committees/projects	$2,046	$–	$–	$1,228	$409	$409
		Totals	$306,900	$60,766	$72,019	$64,040	$67,825	$42,250

Figure 8.3. Process classification by activity.

		Process cost summary					
		Budget $52,657,653		Salaries $44,691,653		Operating budget $7,966,000	
Process code	Process description	Total process cost	% Direct cadet benefit	% Indirect cadet of student activities	% Future academy value-add	% Acad admin	% Non value-add
1	Understand uscg requirements & expectations	$389,474 0.74%	$5,962	$45,686	$214,115	$96,651	$27,059
2	Develop vision & strategy for the academy	$813,652 1.55%	$22,185	$28,515	$451,463	$194,834	$116,655
3	Design programs and training materials	$2,014,872 3.83%	$552,422	$214,176	$727,977	$431,289	$89,008
4	Develop marketing/recruiting strategy	$488,642 0.93%	$18,269	$22,026	$266,451	$114,625	$67,271
5	Identify, recruit & enroll cadets	$2,151,132 4.09%	$600,453	$108,261	$922,490	$418,757	$101,169
6	Deliver academic programs	$10,866,769 20.64%	$7,041,154	$1,377,721	$1,686,168	$548,099	$213,626
7	Develop military knowledge & preparedness	$1,948,208 3.70%	$1,383,351	$188,788	$289,193	$74,063	$12,813

Figure 8.4. Process summary report (continued).

#							
8	Develop & ensure cadet wellness	$6,279,520 11.93%	$5,180,351	$646,221	$176,381	$268,348	$8,218
9	Deliver training programs (ldc)	$511,201 0.97%	$278,938	$45,634	$118,061	$61,788	$6,780
10	Graduate & deploy effective officers	$792,767 1.51%	$323,427	$71,508	$89,877	$245,183	$62,772
11	Develop & manage human resources	$2,939,062 5.58%	$131,324	$834,703	$393,367	$1,268,007	$311,661
12	Manage information	$1,398,218 2.66%	$180,739	$303,269	$252,578	$523,673	$137,960
13	Manage financial and physical resources	$11,944,076 22.68%	$4,609,590	$3,707,617	$1,095,870	$2,042,805	$488,194
14	Manage legal, military & academic records & relationships	$6,033,439 11.46%	$220,532	$1,608,384	$1,850,427	$1,900,493	$453,602
15	Execute outreach/public relations programs	$3,311,819 6.29%	$590,984	$501,197	$1,506,113	$551,215	$162,310
16	Manage improvement & change	$774,804 1.47%	$180,745	$127,813	$373,986	$28,590	$63,669
	Totals	$52,657,653 100.00%	$21,320,427 40.5%	$9,831,519 18.7%	$10,414,517 19.8%	$8,768,421 16.7%	$2,322,768 4.4%

Figure 8.4. Process summary report (continued).

Looking at this example of a process report, we notice that significant funds are used to manage financial and physical resources. The USCGA has a large physical plant, which accounts for some of this challenge. It also has to comply with federal budgeting requirements, which is a time-consuming job that affects every department at the academy. Academic records also consume significant amounts of time and resources, a problem that all academic institutions face. The academy was reviewing different types of software to improve this process at the time of the study. A more efficient and effective software program was identified and implemented, cutting back the time required to maintain academic records. In total, though, at the time of this study it took 50.14% of the academy's resources to manage the educational and institutional processes. This result led to the drive to trim support services and redirect the funds into teaching.

What is interesting when the process approach is added to the data collection is that a process analysis can take place using the information gathered. Specifically, all of the activities that are coded to specific processes or process steps can be separated into reports that lay out all the activities performed for that process (see Figure 8.5). This data can then be directly used to analyze the process to identify gaps and redundancies in the process flow. As noted above, the data also makes it easier to identify and include all the individuals affected by a process flow in any ensuing study, ensuring that all current stakeholders are included in the process redesign effort.

When the process is the focus of the analysis, the summary sheets need to include all of the activities, sorted by process code. It is usually best to put together one report per process so that the data can be analyzed. Once again, this report can easily be generated if a relational database has been created. It can be more time-consuming if a program such as Excel is used. The more complex the organization, the more important it is to use relational structures to make the data usable for process analysis and follow-up activities.

Using VCMS Data to Support Process Improvement

As has been noted above, the VCMS can directly support process improvement projects by presenting the data with process codes and affected

CC	Process code	Activity description	Activity costs	% Direct student benefit	% Indirect support of student activities	% Future academy value-add	% Acad admin	% Non value-add
db	1	Uscg intellectual support	$14,698	$2,940	$2,940	$5,879	$–	$2,940
de	1	Uscg intellectual support	$60,451	$3,023	$24,180	$33,248	$–	$–
f	1	Budget analysis	$46,626	$–	$–	$37,301	$9,325	$–
f	1	Negotiate contracts	$76,687	$–	$–	$38,344	$38,344	$–
f	1	Manage service maintenance agreements	$46,012	$–	$–	$23,006	$23,006	$–
f	1	Seek additional funding	$18,405	$–	$–	$14,724	$1,840	$1,840
s	1	Manage/shape organizational structure	$92,831	$–	$18,566	$37,132	$18,566	$18,566
s	1	Develop justification for future resources	$18,566	$–	$–	$9,283	$5,570	$3,713
			$374,276	$5,962	$45,686	$198,917	$96,651	$27,059

Figure 8.5. Process classification detail.

workgroups attached. This provides the input to the process improvement team. There is more data that can be made available to the improvement team, though. Specifically, the VCMS data also includes the amount of value-add, business value-add, and waste that was identified by participants in the study.

While the waste factor is normally understated in the initial data collection, it at least provides a starting point for setting targets for the improvement team. Since process improvement targets waste and BVA_A tasks that make processes more costly than they need to be, it is useful to have this information available so the improvement team can prioritize the processes they are going to try to improve. Usually one or two processes really stand out, as did the "manage physical and financial resources" process at the USCGA. Clearly, this is the most costly area for the academy, and one that only indirectly affects a portion of the quality of education—maintaining and improving the classrooms. The money spent to comply with federal regulations does not benefit the students at all—it is truly wasted resources when the student perspective is taken.

Summary

This chapter has emphasized the linkage of the VCMS to the process management initiative in an organization. Building from the process framework, such as the one suggested by the APQC Process Framework, the VCMS can collect process data while undertaking the data collection effort. It is important to have the framework complete before VCMS data collection begins. The resulting information should include the workgroup for each activity so that downstream sorting can be completed effectively.

So how can VCMS data support process improvement efforts? The various ways that this can happen include the following:

- Prioritizing process improvement efforts.
- Identifying those work groups or departments that participate in a process.
- Setting improvement targets based on the amount of BVA_A and waste reported.

- Identifying gaps and redundancies in the process flows.
- Gaining an understanding of how much the organization is spending to simply maintain its own internal records.
- Identifying areas where automation and new software may be needed.
- Providing a basic process structure to support improvement efforts.
- Tying process steps to the value attributes that customers care about.
- Separating total costs of a process into value-add, business value-add, and waste.

The VCMS is a constructive way to provide financial support to the process improvement effort. These are complementary efforts, both being focused on maximizing the amount of value created for customers with an organization's limited resources. When used together, the information for both systems tends to improve over time as people become more comfortable with exactly how the data is going to be used. Putting value attributes into the process improvement effort ensures that a more precise picture of how and where customer value is created results.

Everything is connected…no one thing can change by itself.
Paul Hawken[5]

CHAPTER 9

Using VCMS in a Job Shop

To keep our faces toward change and behave like free
spirits in the presence of fate is strength undefeatable.
Helen Keller[1]

It is often noted that there are very few modern models that work as well in service companies as they do in manufacturing firms. The value-based cost management system (VCMS) is an exception to this rule—it works equally well in both settings and it is often easier to implement in service organizations. The reason for this is that the VCMS does not use cost drivers, so there is no need to worry about the challenge of measuring the outcome of a service in a definable way. Since the analysis emphasizes activities and value attributes rather than activity drivers, it can manage service-based data with ease. Some of the best implementations of the VCMS have been in service firms that operate as job shops.

In this chapter, we focus on job shop structures and how they can use the information generated by the VCMS to discipline the spending on a specific customer's job. Since customization of service is sometimes a key to increased customer satisfaction and loyalty, it can serve as a valuable tool to help a job shop retain its current customers and gain new ones. Putting the customer in the driver's seat in defining the activities they want performed for them immediately can make the customer feel as though their unique needs are being met. It is a recipe for success. It is a process that starts with explaining to customers what the VCMS means to them, continues with using the information gathered from customers to discipline the spending in the organization, and ends with reporting back to customers that their money has been spent as they wanted it to be. Let's start with explaining the VCMS to customers.

Explaining the VCMS to Customers

Most customers know what they are expecting from a company when they purchase its services. They can identify value attributes and create their unique value proposition with little prompting from the sales force. The key point to understand is what the customers want versus what value attributes the company is currently able to provide. A systematic customer value analysis such as conjoint analysis will provide an opportunity for customers to make choices between products that are similar and will lead to a result where the importance of the various attributes in customer decision-making process is clear. Remember, though, to support the VCMS, the sum of all the value attributes has to add up to 100%.

The attribute data and their importance in choices made by customers can be collected in a survey type of format, or sometimes by presenting customers with choices between sets of similar products, which contain different combinations and levels of attributes. The customer information collected can sometimes be surprising, as we saw at Impact Communications. Returning to the value profiles for the three different customer segments, we see that there are very different expectations in regard to service attributes across customer segments (see Figure 9.1). For instance, the data suggests that publicity clients place 60% of their value for an engagement on getting placements, while research clients place no value on this attribute. Without customer data, a firm can end up with a generic service strategy for all its clients. Since this is not the best strategy in this case, using the VCMS to ensure that each customer segment can have the type of activities and outcomes that they most desire can be critical for competitive survival and success.

Value attribute	Publicity clients	Marketing services clients	Strategy/research clients
Placements quantity	60%	30%	0%
Creative/proactive service	15%	10%	20%
Strategy/brand service	5%	20%	60%
Knowledge of business	10%	20%	5%
Reputation	5%	5%	10%
Results merchandising	5%	15%	5%
Total	100%	100%	100%

Figure 9.1. Impact communications' value propositions.

A discussion with customers that is centered around value attributes signals the fact that the company's goal is truly to become customer-driven. It is important that the value attribute data collection instrument includes and properly defines all relevant value attributes. It is often recommended to conduct focus groups with customers in advance of data collection in order to properly identify all attributes in the relevant market. When the original list of attributes was first discussed at Impact Communications, for instance, the results merchandising—the quality of presentation to management that reflected positively on the manager who had chosen Impact—was overlooked. It became obvious that this was missing when customers were first polled for their input. So, a firm always has to be open to the fact that new value attributes may emerge as the industry develops new products and new players enter the market.

It is, in fact, one of the more valuable aspects of using the VCMS that the customer data enters the process explicitly and thereby forces the organization to be externally focused. Incorporating customer data explicitly into the VCMS provides critical education to all stakeholders in the organization about what the market values and how and if attributes and their importance in the product or service is changing. Since customer preferences are a dynamic element in the value creation process, staying in touch with the market using the VCMS as a communications tool is vitally important.

To summarize these points, then, when the salesperson meets with a potential customer to discuss a job or a purchase of goods or services, they should focus on the discussion of value attributes embedded in the product sold and articulate how the specific combination of features provides value to this customer. A service or a product with a different combination and importance of the features needs to be offered to the customer in case the customer belongs to a segment whose valuation of features is different.

Our field work shows that the VCMS model fosters effective communication between the salesperson and the customers in regard to the value attributes delivered rather than incentivizing the salesperson to solely compete on price. The VCMS model creates a new language for communicating with customers that expands beyond simple task or activity offerings to a deeper understanding of the value profile—what will make the customer happy with the outcomes of the engagement.

Value attribute	Customer weighting
Professional advice	
Accurate analysis	
Research quality	
Responsiveness	
Reputation	
Understanding of needs	
Reasonable fees	
Communication of results	
Other _____	
	100%

Figure 9.2. Example of a value attribute listing.

Creating a Job-Specific Value Profile

Having gathered the customer data, the organization next needs to develop a job-specific value profile. This profile is as important as the physical description of the work to be completed because it directs attention to exactly what the customer (or a segment) expects from the organization. It defines best practice for a successful job. Figure 9.2 shows an example of value attributes in an accounting firm, where each client has different needs.

Some clients of an accounting firm are most concerned with the advice and reputation of the firm, while others place more importance on reasonable fees and accurate analysis. Each engagement is likely different, with clients placing more or less weight on these various attributes. And, some customers may add things such as friendly service to this list. The final list of value attributes and weightings depends on how each customer views their relationship with the firm.

Directing Resources Where They Matter

Once the value profile has been collected for a specific customer, it comes back to the firm to guide the engagement planning process. If the customer cares about friendly service, it may suggest that an accountant that is more outgoing might be chosen to be the direct contact for the customer. The engagement has to be planned so that the resources of the firm are directed toward the things that matter most to the customer. Since probably all customers of an accounting firm expect accurate analysis, it goes without saying that the job plan should ensure that the right people are assigned to the tasks that need to be completed. A partner may be chosen as the direct contact for the customer, signaling to the customer that their job is important to the firm.

The resources must be planned, then, to ensure that the customer value proposition is met. For Impact Communications, this meant that many more people had to be assigned to the basic "dial and smile" activities required to gain placements since publicity clients were a majority of the firm's business and this is what they valued. It was a culture change for the organization, where a successful career path in the past had been to avoid direct publicity placements activities and to emphasize research tasks. In this case, this was what the founder valued, but not what was found to be valued by the publicity customers. When company resources are aligned with customer preferences, a reconfiguration of internal processes might be required so that the right attributes are delivered in every job. It doesn't matter what the firm cares most about—it is customer preferences that should drive performance.

Keeping Tabs on Spending

Once the job has been planned and resources assigned, a tracking system needs to be put in place that ensures that the customer's value profile is used to prioritize actions and resource use for each job. This means that the VCMS becomes part of the organization's management control system, being used to evaluate the success of jobs and the efforts of the managers who run them.

Let's return to our accounting firm example and look at how this type of reporting mechanism might be set up (see Figure 9.3). As you can see, the engagement dollars have been split up amongst the value attributes, creating the revenue equivalents that drive the model. A cost projection has then been developed, ensuring that the engagement is profitable. Company expectations for this engagement, given the level of competition in the industry and given its customer value in the market, is that

Value attribute	Customer weighting	Revenue equivalent	Desired cost	Actual spending
Professional advice	10%	$1,000	$500	
Accurate analysis	40%	$4,000	$2,000	
Research quality	5%	$500	$250	
Responsiveness	10%	$1,000	$500	
Reputation	5%	$500	$250	
Understanding of needs	10%	$1,000	$500	
Reasonable fees	15%	$1,500	$750	
Communication of results	5%	$500	$250	
Other _____				
Administration			$2,500	
	100%		$7,500	

Figure 9.3. Putting resources where customers want them.

50% of the spending should be directed to the value profile, leaving 25% for administration and 25% for profit. The engagement is estimated to be worth $10,000. This report would be used as a guide to the project manager, ensuring that the funds get spent in line with customer needs and their defined value.

The question that naturally comes to mind is how to match the activities that are being performed to these value attributes. This is where it is important to have completed the VCMS study inside the firm. The results of that study can create a taxonomy of activities that are classified by value attribute. For reasonable fees, which serve as a table stakes issue, the decision might be made to add this dollar amount ($750) to the accuracy attribute as this is a basic feature expected of all well-run accounting engagements. It could also be spread across several attributes if that is deemed to be the basic features an engagement should have.

With the communication attribute, the billings that align with client meetings would be mapped there. Individuals engaged on a specific job would then use the activity taxonomy to bill their hours to attributes. Anything that is done that doesn't pass the value-add test during the VCMS internal study would be charged to administration. Clearly, if too much of the total cost ends up in administration, the job won't earn its targeted 25% profit.

The entire point of this discussion is that the original VCMS study provides a list of value-adding activities by value attribute. It even goes so far as to split an activity out against multiple attributes. Internal personnel have to become conversant with this activity list and be able to use it to make judgments about how much time and resources should be dedicated to specific tasks. The VCMS approach, then, replaces traditional engagement budgeting, substituting a customer-driven approach for one that is firm-defined.

Reporting Back to Customers

Closing the loop on a customer-driven job structure requires that the firm report back to customers about where spending is taking place. Here we return to the original percentages and use the internal tracking information to match spending against the defined value attributes. This is what was done at Impact Communications. For our accounting firm example, the report back to the customer might look like the following (see Figure 9.4).

It is clear that in this engagement, more time has been spent providing professional advice to the customer and actually performing the engagement calculations and worksheets than were originally planned. The shortfall on reputation can be explained by noting that this engagement required more hands-on than planned, which might mean that the reputation of

Value attribute	Customer weighting	Actual spending	Spending gap
Professional advice	10%	15%	+5%
Accurate analysis	40%	45%	+5%
Research quality	5%	4%	−1%
Responsiveness	10%	11%	+1%
Reputation	5%	2%	−3%
Understanding of needs	10%	12%	+2%
Reasonable fees	15%	13%	−2%
Communication of results	5%	6%	+1%
Other _____			
	100%	108%	+8%

Figure 9.4. Reporting back to customers.

the firm should be positively impacted if the customer is pleased with the outcomes—the related value multiplier should go up. Six percent more time has been spent in direct communications (professional advice and communication of results) than planned, suggesting that the customer may have understated how much interaction they desired on the job. For research quality, the engagement may have proven to be easier than originally planned, requiring less research to result in a positive outcome.

These calculations are made using the internal reports and calculating the percentage of spending by category as a percent of the total nonadministrative tasks. Since this was planned originally to be 50% of the total spend, it is clear that this job made 4% less profit than planned. Why 4%? The percentages reported back to the customer are against the 50% benchmark, so an 8% overage actually converts to only 4% of the job's total. As long as administration didn't exceed its 25% target, the job should be profitable.

If the client is happy with the service received, the job report should help provide input to the next engagement between the firm and the customer. Both sides of the client–firm relationship learn from this process, gaining a better understanding of what the customer really wants in a successful engagement. It is clear that this customer wants more communication than was originally planned, so future engagements should budget more time for this important activity. The completed job reporting package shows the customer that the firm is listening, and also that their preferences may be slightly different than they originally thought if they are satisfied with the job.

What happens if the customer is dissatisfied with the outcomes of the engagement? The salesperson or partner, whoever is doing the debriefing at the end of the job, needs to isolate exactly what the customer didn't value. Perhaps they wanted even more direct communication. In that case, the firm might need to enlist a staff accountant to do some of the communication as their billing rate would be lower, keeping the job within its price structure while increasing the intensity of communications. The whole point is that there is now precise information that can be used in planning future engagements to bring them closer to delivering the right level of customer value. It is a communication process and a learning process, one that begins and ends with direct communication with the customer.

Assessing the Impact of VCMS-driven Customer Support

In marketing, loyalty of a customer is often recognized as one of the important aspects of an organization's relationship with its customers. Loyal customers do repeat business with the firm, increasing the profitability of jobs as the firm learns how to meet customer expectations in more efficient and effective ways. So, one possible way to assess the impact of VCMS-driven customer support is through changes in the loyalty ratings for the firm's customer base.

Why does loyalty matter? The answer to this lies in the amount of money that is spent to gain a new customer. It often takes significant financial and other investments to acquire a new customer. All of these costs have to be borne by the jobs the firm secures from the customer. If there is only one job secured because the customer was dissatisfied with the outcome, then all of this cost has to be borne by one job, quite likely turning it from a profitable engagement to one where losses occur. This was the situation facing Impact Communications before they turned to the VCMS approach to plan and monitor their performance on specific engagements.

So, connecting the impact of the VCMS approach with customer loyalty and satisfaction is a recommended step in ensuring that performance and profit improvements are attained by the organization. Monitoring every job to ensure that spending corresponds as closely as possible to the predefined customer expectations is critical. Adjusting expectations as more data become available is also important. The VCMS is a learning system, one where the firm is constantly absorbing more data about how its work affects the value proposition and where the customer comes to better understand what they really expect from the organization.

If job overruns continue, it may be necessary to negotiate changes in the fee structure with the client. These conversations are easier to have when the customer can see that they are actually demanding more service from the firm than was originally planned. This discussion also leaves room for the customer to alter their behavior in order to help the engagement remain on financial track while still providing the desired outcomes. Either way, the VCMS once again serves as a very important communication tool, one that removes ambiguity from the analysis and decisions surrounding a job and explicitly connects customer value with internal resource consumption.

Summary

In this chapter, we have shown how the VCMS can be used to help discipline the planning process and actual activities that take place when a job is taken by a job-shop firm. Using two examples from service organizations, the discussion provided a look at the engagement document as the first place where the firm and customer come to a clearer definition of what defines success in terms of job completion.

The engagement agreement serves as the basis for planning and monitoring internal activities. Using the VCMS coding scheme originally developed, the firm's employees map their activities against the value attributes defined by customer data. For Impact Communications, we saw that the publicity clients wanted 60% of the effort of the firm to be directed toward gaining publicity placements. Since this had not been the focus of the firm prior to the VCMS study, it required a change in culture and expectations in the firm itself. Since publicity clients were generally leaving the firm after one engagement, there was no loyalty to the firm. This meant that a lot of money was spent getting new customers on an ongoing basis. The VCMS helped diagnose and isolate the cause of this customer churn and provided the organization with a clear path forward. Serving as a communication tool both internally and externally, the VCMS provides a clear signal about how success is defined in an engagement.

The VCMS approach includes the firm reporting back to the customer about how funds were spent on their job. This is a time where communication of satisfaction or concerns can take place, using precise definitions of expectations and actions. Some firms, such as Impact Communications, have developed monthly reports to customers that track the spending to date against the engagement plan. The more communication that takes place between the customer and the firm, the more likely the customer will be satisfied and become a more loyal customer, one who engages the firm multiple times, potentially improving the firm's profit. Customer loyalty is one of the critical measures of an organization's success. Sound, effective communication of expectations and results is the means to this end.

> *Decide what you want, decide what you are willing to exchange for it. Establish your priorities and go to work.*
>
> H. L. Hunt[2]

CHAPTER 10

VCMS and Product/Service Development

*The man who will use his skill and constructive imagination
to see how much he can give for a dollar, instead of how
little he can give for a dollar, is bound to succeed.*

Henry Ford[1]

One of the most important activities of a company is using the profit earned in the market to develop new products and services that bring future sales into the company. As we've seen, the value-based cost management system (VCMS) captures this investment from across the organization with BVA_F, or Business value-add—Future. The VCMS has even more power, though, helping to focus spending based on customer-defined preferences and supporting the costing exercise that is critical to new product development. Clearly, the costing exercise can be supported by any well-developed cost management system, but only the VCMS allows costs to be prioritized based on how closely they map to future customer value creation.

In this chapter we focus on the development efforts of three of the companies where VCMS field work was performed—Universal Lifts, Windows, Inc., and Frangor. In the first two cases, a new product launch was supported by the VCMS. At Frangor, the augmentation of service responsiveness resulted from the study. In all of these cases, the VCMS provided support for understanding the development costs and also the potential value-added proportion of total costs. Using an incremental costing framework, these new product/service offerings were changed as a result of the supporting analysis. Let's turn to the facts of these three cases to see what happened.

Value Engineering and VCMS

Value engineering entails the use of customer value data in the design and development of a product or service. We saw how Impact Communications changed its job management approach using customer input—it was a service that was modified based on the value creation model. Value engineering is most often used for tangible products, such as automobiles and machines, but it can be applied anytime a product or service is being developed with customer input as the driving force.

What has been learned through the value engineering logic is that fully 90% of the cost of a product or service over its lifetime is locked in at the development stage.[2] This fact was laid out in the CAM-I[3] conceptual design as a vital new piece of information. Why is design so important? The design of the product locks in place the components that will be needed, the assembly sequence, and the type of support processes that will be required to make the product/service bundle attractive to customers. It ties the product to a certain internal build structure and often defines the amount of administrative work that will be used in its maintenance.

The VCMS ties to the value engineering exercise by laying out the structure in terms of what level of value-add is going to be possible given the structure of the firm. It places a value on the attributes in terms of revenue equivalents and then compares the current projected costs to these revenue equivalents to get prelaunch multipliers. If the design is too heavy on one value attribute, say colors available, over another, the multipliers will be low for this attribute. This is an important signal that provides diagnostics on where the value engineering analysis should focus to take cost and waste out of the production process. It can also signal where not enough value has been built into the product if a value multiplier is too high. In the constant give-and-take of the value engineering design process, customer input is used to drive the design process and influence important decisions that will ultimately spell the success or failure of the new product launch. It is a critical function, one that needs to be completed with care to ensure the product meets customer expectations.

At one site, Universal Lifts, value engineering was not done on the launch of a new lifting device for automobiles being serviced in a garage. Replacing the sunk bays that had hydraulic lifts that had high propensity to leak, causing environmental problems, these free-standing above ground lifts were seen as a major innovation in the lift industry. Unfortunately, so much value was built into the product that it ended up costing more to make the product than the market price would bear. Customers were very satisfied with the product, but the company lost money on every lift made. And, as noted above, 90% of this cost was locked in by the design, so there was very little that could be done *ex post*, except to identify the sources of major design problems.

Universal Lifts ended up pulling the plug on the first above ground lift and then going back to the drawing board, this time using value engineering to design a new lift that met customer needs but could be sold at a profit. Re-launching the product line allowed adjustments in both features and price, resulting in a redesigned product that generated a profit for the company. The new design was limited, though, to the machinery that had been purchased for the first above ground lift, making even the redesigned product more expensive than it would have been if value engineering had driven the design from the inception. Old problems were brought forward, but managed in a different way to reduce some of the cost that was embedded in the product.

Avoiding these types of problems is one of the driving forces behind value engineering efforts. Finding out once a product is launched that it cannot possibly make money for the company is not a good option—it was a recipe for disaster that this medium-sized manufacturer barely survived. Putting the customer value first in the design process, using constant customer feedback when design decisions are being made, and keeping an eye on the costs to meet customer expectations are at the heart of value engineering. While a product or service is in the design phase, changes can be made to drive costs out and focus the final offering on those attributes customers care about. It is the most logical way to approach product/service development.

Gaining Customer Input—Windows, Inc.

When Windows, Inc. decided it wanted to launch a less expensive line of windows to meet competition in the replacement window market, it turned to customer data to gain information. As was shown earlier in this book, the company research showed that it had three primary customers for its products—homeowners, small builders, and architects. The preliminary readings from the brand pulse analysis are detailed in Figure 10.1.

In this field work it was discovered that there were some very different preferences for the final product across segments. Specifically, there were many costs that had to be incurred to provide value for the architects and small builders that the final consumer—the homeowner—did not value. We have talked about this problem before, noting that the costs incurred to support an industry value chain actually come out of the end-firm's profits because the final product's value in terms of revenue earned is determined by customers. The final customer may not care about such things as distribution and ease of assembly. They may be paying the builder for these services. The builder charges for assembling the window, but the final customer doesn't really care who does this task—it is assumed that basic functionality as defined by the competitive market price incorporates all the nondifferentiating features of a window.

In this brand-based marketing study, price was the major attribute. Since this window was designed and produced to fill the commodity

Attribute	Small builders	Architects	Home owners	Weighted average
Brand	11	7	6	8
Warranty	10	6	6	7
Distribution	8			2
Assembly	9			3
Sizes	10			3
Price	52	48	47	49
Cleaning		4	5	3
Durability		7	7	5
Appearance		7	7	5
Weather tightness		7	8	6
Operation		6	6	4
Efficiency		8	8	6
Total %	100	100	100	100

Figure 10.1. Customer value attributes.

market niche, most of its value was captured by the price, or table stakes attribute. This indicated that there was a significant bundle of functions provided in the market by many other suppliers of windows. Interestingly, the final consumer did not place any value on sizes available. It was simply assumed that standard sizes would exist that would fit their needs—size was part of table stakes for consumers. The final list of customer-defined attributes was large compared to many identified in the study, but reflected the high risk nature of this type of purchase.

This data was then used to develop revenue equivalents, as shown in Figure 10.2. Here you see conditional weights, which are the weightings in terms of how important the particular stakeholders' expectations are to the value profile of the final product. The projected revenues for each of the value attributes was then used to guide the development process using VCMS-supported value engineering to gain a solid understanding of how much it would cost to provide the desired attribute. Once again, delivering a product that meets the competitive standard is of utmost importance to the customers. Interestingly, the builder didn't seem to care about attributes that were deemed critical by the homeowner, such as weather-tightness. To the builder this was a table stakes issue, to the homeowner and architect segment it was an attribute that provided differentiation and opportunity for receiving additional value.

What was interesting in the Windows, Inc. field study was that the marketing data used was modified after it was collected to make it fit the VCMS' structural requirement that the weightings add up to 100%. The customer segment value data provided by marketing were complemented by additional information containing customer segment attribute valuation. Each attribute's weight was then divided by the total, transforming the results into the table above. It was interesting that some of the attributes that had been included in the marketing analysis "fell off the table" when converted—they simply weren't very important in the overall delivery of customer value. This result provided valuable information for Windows, Inc., which was ultimately used to discipline the value engineering process.

The results of the cost analysis are provided in Figure 10.3. Here we observe that the profit required was first taken out, resulting in an allowable cost. This was then divided by the number of units projected to

	Consumer weight	Consumer wondit'l	Architect weight	Architect condit'l	Builder weight	Builder condit'l	Total weight	Revenue equivalent
				Custom builder value analysis				
Brand	5.0%	2.5%	7.0%	0.7%	10.0%	4.0%	7.2%	$12,587,400
Warranty	6.0%	3.0%	6.0%	0.6%	9.0%	3.6%	7.2%	$12,587,400
Cleaning	4.0%	2.0%	4.0%	0.4%		0.0%	2.4%	$4,195,800
Durability	6.0%	3.0%	7.0%	0.7%		0.0%	3.7%	$6,468,525
Appear.	6.0%	3.0%	7.0%	0.7%		0.0%	3.7%	$6,468,525
Wthr-tght	7.0%	3.5%	7.0%	0.7%		0.0%	4.2%	$7,342,650
Operation	5.0%	2.5%	6.0%	0.6%		0.0%	3.1%	$5,419,575
Efficiency	8.0%	4.0%	8.0%	0.8%		0.0%	4.8%	$8,391,600
Price	53.0%	26.5%	48.0%	4.8%	54.0%	21.6%	52.9%	$92,482,425
Dist'n					8.0%	3.2%	3.2%	$5,594,400
Ass'y					9.0%	3.6%	3.6%	$6,293,700
Sizes					10.0%	4.0%	4.0%	$6,993,000
	100.0%	50.0%	100.0%	10.0%	100.0%	40.0%	100.0%	$174,825,000

Figure 10.2. Revenue equivalents for Windows, Inc.

Target cost breakdown–unitized

Attribute	Wted value**	Revenue estimate–year 2003	Profit holdback	Cost limit	Cost limit per unit	Value-added cost (27%)	BVA-current cost (11%)	BVA-future cost (11%)	BVA-admin. cost (24%)	Waste (27%)
Price*	59	$127,558,000	$25,511,600	$102,046,400	$57.98	$15.65	$6.38	$6.38	$13.92	$15.65
Options (color/grilles)	8	$17,296,000	$3,459,200	$13,836,800	$7.86	$2.12	$0.86	$0.86	$1.89	$2.12
Appearance	6	$12,972,000	$2,594,400	$10,377,600	$5.90	$1.59	$0.65	$0.65	$1.42	$1.59
Brand	9	$19,458,000	$3,891,600	$15,566,400	$8.84	$2.39	$0.97	$0.97	$2.12	$2.39
Warranty/Durability	12	$25,944,000	$5,188,800	$20,755,200	$11.79	$3.18	$1.30	$1.30	$2.83	$3.18
Sizing grid	6	$12,972,000	$2,594,400	$10,377,600	$5.90	$1.59	$0.65	$0.65	$1.42	$1.59
Total	100	$216,200,000	$43,240,000	$172,960,000	$98.27	$26.53	$10.81	$10.81	$23.59	$26.53

Figure 10.3. VCMS target costing structure for Windows, Inc.

be sold to calculate a value-add profile, or target cost, for the proposed window. Once again, some attributes were removed from the analysis as this was focused solely on the consumer, not the trading partners that had been included in the earlier studies. Trading partner costs would need to come out of BVA-Administrative. The design process itself, including the marketing studies, comprised the BVA-Future in the study, providing a discipline on the costs of actually designing the product. The limits by cost category were set based both on what management felt was reasonable and results of the internal VCMS study.

This was one of the first organizations where VCMS was used to insert discipline into the product/service development process. It was natural to use the target costing approach, where the target price is reduced by desired profit to get the allowable cost for a unit. Actual costs could then be compared to this set of targets to determine where cost cutting in the design process needed to take place. It was in this field study where table stakes began to take on meaning. Adding such things as weather-tightness to the table stakes area helped reduce the number of attributes that the company had to manage in designing its new window line. And, as is common with all target costing exercises, the first design did not meet its targeted cost projections. This is where value engineering and the VCMS come together—to bring the costs down to attributes that the engineers can actually use to make adjustments to the design before the product launches.

One of the interesting findings of this field study was that some attributes served a larger role in the development of a potential customer than they did in the final sale. Customers usually buy an entire system of windows and doors when they remodel their homes. When they first look at windows, they want to have lots of options for color and shape, for instance. But, when the final buying decision occurs, the majority of the market prefers standard windows with white trim.

Windows, Inc. had to be able to offer variety to the customer even if very few ever decided on purchasing the options offered. The risk of failing to make variety available was a potential loss of sales of an entire system of doors and windows. That means the value attributes used in creating a list of potential suppliers is different from that used in the final decision, a lesson that had profound implications for the new product launch. Meeting trading partner demands added cost to the final product design that most likely would not be recouped downstream through actual sales.

The Cost of Support

What can also be seen in the Windows, Inc. example in Figure 10.3 is that the cost of support is recognized when a VCMS approach is taken. This can sometimes be overlooked in the design process, resulting in reduced profits once the product actually launches. Unless some tool or approach is used that specifically recognizes that back office functions also are impacted by a new product launch, they can be overlooked. The cost of support includes the business-to-business costs that the final consumer is unwilling to pay for in setting a market price on a good. These costs can be hidden in a flat charge of overhead to a project if a purely engineering approach is taken.

This is the crux of the matter. Support costs occur in all organizations—they cannot be avoided. The question is are they covered in a flat charge for overhead that probably distorts the actual costs of a specific product or service support functions or are they traced to specific outcomes? In most firms, the overhead approach is taken. Many years of activity-based costing research, though, have underscored the fact that products don't use support processes to the same degree. The higher the degree of variety in a product line, for instance, the more likely it is to require more support work.

If the costs of this support work are made visible through a system such as the VCMS, using a process framework, as much attention can be paid to the development of support processes as is paid to the design and development of the product itself. There are better and worse ways to provide support. It is important that support processes be defined, measured, and controlled as tightly as product/service costs are measured.

Without this level of attention, total costs can grow out of control as supporting the actual value-added work becomes more and more complex, increasing haphazardly through the budgeting process. Using the VCMS to monitor and control these expenditures before they take place is the only way to ensure that the organization's profits don't become the victim of poor support process performance. As was the case in Windows,

Inc. the VCMS target costing exercise identified an acceptable level of support cost as well as value-added costs. This is the recipe for success in the design and development of a product or service.

Extending the Service Profile

As has been noted in earlier chapters, the VCMS approach works very well in service settings. This means that when the service profile of a company needs to be changed or perhaps even developed as a result of changes in market trends or customer preferences, the VCMS can be used in the same way as it was at Windows, Inc. An example of this occurred at Frangor, a company discussed in Chapter 5. The company focused on its manufacturing base, not investing enough time and effort into its service support processes. Once the VCMS study was completed, it became very clear that that customer really cared about timely customer assistance when a machine went down. Customers valued quick service very highly as a result of tremendous cost of a malfunctioning machine in the middle of the harvesting season.

Frangor took the information from the VCMS study and developed a new service profile for the company, including an estimate of how much of the price being paid for products was actually earned by the service function. Instead of waiting one or more weeks for service, management put in place a highly responsive repair network including parts distribution that could get a broken tractor or other farm implement back up and running in hours rather than weeks.

This change greatly improved the competitiveness of Frangor in the farming implements market in Italy, where small machines are needed due to space constraints and farm sizes in terms of both land and maneuvering room. It was a prime example of how the VCMS can guide a company to improve its processes or, in this case, redevelop its service delivery and improve its position in the market. By putting a dollar amount on the service component, management could estimate how much it should be spending on this important activity.

Don't Ignore the Hidden Waste

As has been noted earlier, one of the primary challenges when implementing the VCMS in any setting is that employees may be hesitant to identify any level of waste in their operations. This may be especially true during the development phase, when designers and engineers are thinking that they are putting together flawless processes and products. As was seen at Windows, Inc. there was waste in the newly designed product. This waste is normally in the administrative areas, but it can also be in the design itself, as we saw with Universal Lifts. When products are designed without careful attention being paid to the processes that are used to produce them, waste may enter every step of the product.

At Universal Lifts, the traditional processes for making a lift were streamlined, but when the new plant was constructed the lessons learned from earlier development projects was ignored. The product was moved during construction multiple times, which given the size and weight of the component parts created unnecessary processes and activities. This embedded waste was eliminated when the product and supporting processes were redesigned, but this redesign took away valuable funds that could have been used elsewhere in the organization.

Waste also occurs in the support processes that the new product or service uses. Usually little or no attention is paid to the impact of the new product on support processes, where wasteful activities may already abound. These hidden pockets of waste rob the firm of its profitability and are often overlooked during the target costing phase of the analysis. How and where components are sourced, for instance, can have a major impact on the costs of the company when developing a new product. If price rather than effectiveness drives the purchase decision, the organization can be burdened with excess inventories that were bought in bulk to gain a purchase price savings. This inventory may clog up the plant floor and take away important resources from other purposes.

Using the VCMS approach, the entire set of processes required to support the launch of a product is documented. This documentation means that the designers know what is currently done in the support area and can make suggestions for changes that might better meet the needs of the new product or service. They can also factor in the costs of this service with more than a general overhead charge, which is otherwise how these support activities are included in the estimated cost. A full bill of activities can be developed and the level of recorded waste in these activities acknowledged early in the design process. Fixing broken support processes is one of the side benefits of a VCMS-focused development project. Making the hidden waste visible means that it will be acted upon, with the entire organization benefitting, not just the new product. Designing in excellence in operations has to extend to the entire support system of the organization.

Summary

In this chapter we've seen how the VCMS can be used to support the development of a new product or service. At Windows, Inc., the marketing study data was transformed through a simple weighting approach to show the value profiles of the three customers segments—small builders, architects, and the ultimate consumer. While the business-to-business expenses were all BVA-Administrative costs, at least the company had an idea of what level of investment would be needed to serve their trading partners. The VCMS data helped focus the design process, ensuring that the final product met customer expectations.

At Frangor we learned that an entire service support system was redesigned once the VCMS had identified how much of the revenue the company was receiving for its products was actually tied to post-purchase service support. Using this information, improvements were made both in the product manufacturing process (to reduce costs) and in the service support area. A new service process was developed that was far more responsive, earning Frangor a competitive advantage in the relevant farm implements market. Without the VCMS data, this shortfall in meeting customer expectations would not have been recognized or as clearly defined in monetary terms.

The VCMS, then, places dollar amounts on specific aspects of a product or service during the design phase that can be used to discipline the development process. Instead of adding features to products because the company is capable of doing so, a company adds features when these are valued and desired by customers. In this manner the VCMS is linked to the two most valuable tools used in product/service development efforts—value engineering and target costing. The VCMS helps focus these efforts using revenue equivalents and projected direct and indirect costs to keep everyone's eyes on the total impact of the new product or service on the company's manufacturing and support processes. The VCMS makes key value attributes more visible, and hence actionable, in the organization.

> *Knowledge and human power are synonymous, since the ignorance*
> *of the cause frustrates the effect.*
>
> Lord Bacon[4]

CHAPTER 11

Building VCMS
in to the Organization

Method is like packing things in a box; a good packer
will get in half as much again as a bad one.

Cecil[1]

One of the major challenges in any new approach to managing an organization is the decision to build the new information into the ongoing information system or to simply use it as a study that provides new insights. In the case of the value-based cost management system (VCMS), it makes the most sense to build it in because the VCMS keeps important information for strategic and incremental analysis current and ready to use in a variety of decision settings. Creating an actionable basis for making changes to the organization, the VCMS provides all of the benefits of activity-based costing with the additional insights that are provided by tying activities to specific value attributes. It is a comprehensive cost analysis tool.

The VCMS has been used for different purposes by the companies that have been studied in our field work. Since each site was unique, with specific problems that needed to be addressed, the model has been tested in a wide variety of situations and found to be useful. Let's look at some of the evidence of VCMS usefulness from our field work.

Strategic Analysis and the VCMS

The VCMS model is a strategic tool first and foremost. Providing a mapping of the company's efforts against the value attributes preferred by customers, it helps direct attention to those areas where the firm is under- or over-performing. The result is a more tightly defined set of change actions that are needed to improve a firm's competitiveness.

Frangor was one of the early implementations of our model. A farm implements manufacturer in Italy, it employed strategic cost analysis to help it understand its overall position in the industry. This information was useful, but was not as actionable as the company had hoped. It then turned to the VCMS to gain a more precise understanding of where and how the firm was meeting customer needs and where it was falling short. As can be seen in Figure 11.1, our work identified two customer segments using data collected with customer surveys. Additionally, what Frangor's customers valued did not correspond to attributes identified by management as most important, making this valuable new information for the firm and its decision-making.

Looking at the information in Figure 11.1, we see that across the board management did not have a good understanding of the value profile for their company. The fact that two segments were identified had also eluded the company during the years. Since each segment wanted and valued different attributes, it made it quite a challenge for the firm. Should they focus on the price-sensitive customers and change their current differentiation strategy to a price strategy, or should they continue to differentiate themselves, placing more emphasis on service reliability and customer assistance than they did in the past? The decision was made to enhance service and also to look within the firm to try to find ways to reduce costs so they could also be more price-competitive.

Value attributes	Total market profile	Customers cluster profile		Management customer profile
		Price sensitive	Service sensitive	
Technical reliability	21%	16%	24%	15%
Price	14%	37%	5%	30%
Service reliability	20%	12%	21%	15%
Durability	15%	16%	15%	20%
Customer assistance	20%	4%	24%	10%
Technical performance	10%	15%	11%	10%
Total	100%	100%	100%	100%

Figure 11.1. Frangor's value profiles.

Based on this information, changes were made to the design and development process to focus on a family of products using one stable platform rather than the one-up designs that had been developed in the past. This allowed the company to cut its inventory of raw materials by one-third, a major cost reduction. A second change was described in Chapter 10. The firm invested more in its service profile so that they could meet the demands of the service-sensitive customers. Not all customers would place equal value on service, but in a differentiation strategy it was critical that Frangor choose a path that would separate them from their major competitors who were competing predominantly on cost.

In strategic analysis, then, the VCMS model helps the company understand the differences in attributes valued by customer segments and what path forward makes the most sense. Since a differentiation strategy allows the company more room to innovate, it is often preferred once customer data enters the analysis. Competing on cost constantly pushes the profit margins of the firm, placing ever greater pressure on finding waste and BVA-Administrative costs and removing or limiting them. The firm that uses VCMS as their strategic model knows where not to cut costs—they protect value-add and BVA-Future expenditures. This makes cost cutting a surgical rather than a chainsaw operation.

This was the experience at Windows, Inc. also, as noted in Chapter 10. They found that there were differences in the preferences between their trading partners and the final customer. Since the costs created by the trading partners were not truly value-add in nature, but more likely BVA-Administrative, there was significant impetus to find a way to meet trading partner requests with minimal outlay of new funds.

We've also seen that Impact Communications had a significant strategic revelation when using the VCMS approach. They found out that they had three very different segments of customers, and they were only servicing one segment well. This led to changes in the way jobs were designed and executed. The VCMS-based information also led to internal structural changes in the firm, with the pure publicity work (smile and dial) being placed higher in importance than the research work that only a small segment of its customer population valued.

GTI made major changes in its strategic profile once it realized that a large proportion of its total income and profit were coming from traditional "dial tone is great" customers. The company had been trying to compete with Internet providers and spending less and less time and money servicing its basic customers. The company was ultimately bought out by a major phone service provider, where the major investments necessary to thrive in the Internet-dominated market could be justified based on scale. For a small local telephone company, though, the profits simply weren't there. At the time of the study, basic services for basic customers was the source of majority of its profit. It was a lesson in not taking the loyal customer for granted.

Identifying the value profile of different customer segments is one of the primary benefits of the VCMS approach. Tying the company's costs to the value profile is an added benefit, one that allows for targeted changes in the way the company is managed. It helps make the decisions that management undertakes have a greater focus and become more reflective of what the market really wants from their product or service. And, for a trading partner farther back in the value stream, it helps them better understand what elements of their work contribute to the value of the final product—communication is enhanced because it is built on customer value data, not management opinion or perception of customer wants.

The VCMS, then, is a valuable strategic tool, one that can be used on an ongoing basis to track the preferences of customers in the marketplace and to keep the firm constantly fine-tuning its operations to better meet these expectations. It is a growth-oriented model because it emphasizes removing waste and reducing the cost of BVA-administrative tasks, refocusing the savings into areas the customer values. The result is a multiplication of the value delivered by the firm and the enhancement of its strategic position. In every firm that employed the VCMS, then, improved strategic decision-making was the result of the pilot study. The proof that VCMS is a strategic tool lies in the results of this fieldwork.

Incremental Analysis and the VCMS

There has also been a significant use of the information acquired during the VCMS study to support incremental analysis in the firms that have been studied. Incremental analysis is short-term operational analysis that emphasizes making shifts to how work is currently being done. For instance, Frangor used the results of the study to determine whether or not it should directly manufacture more of the parts that went into its farm implements. The company had traditionally been a final assembly shop, outsourcing all of its parts to other manufacturers. This placed it in a profit squeeze situation, where suppliers would raise their prices but Frangor couldn't simply pass these price increases along. Making more parts allowed Frangor to recoup more of the profits that came from their final products. It was a decision based on VCMS information.

At Easy Air, an entire study of the impact of long haul flights on overall costs and profits of the firm was completed. Figure 11.2 shows part of how this analysis was done. The shaded data boxes were where management could made changes to model assumptions, while the unshaded boxes were calculated based on the results of the activity analysis underlying the VCMS approach. Several revenue and cost scenarios were developed as part of the study, resulting in a change to the structure of the sector model used to schedule the planes. Specifically, the long haul flights were made into a separate sector, resulting in changes in management of that segment of flights. Decoupling the long haul flights from the regional networks reduced the impact of variation in the long haul operations on the effectiveness and efficiency of the short haul regional networks.

This effort resulting in an operational a change that helped the company improve its on-time performance statistics, an important measure of quality of service in the airline industry. It was also an illustration of the value of keeping the VCMS data current. With current information, the study could automatically estimate the impact of changes to the operational assumptions of the firm. This was a result of the VCMS being based in activity-based analysis, while not going to the level of activity-based costing. Since activity-based costing estimates assume a volume, it was important to separate the analysis of costs from existing activities and simply make estimates of how much impact the change would have on the capacity available.

At Windows, Inc. the entire management of vacuum-forming some of the window components came under study due to the VCMS analysis. Since capacity cost analysis[2] was used to conduct the costing of the machine centers in the company, very precise data was available to analyze

| | | | | | | | | | | Easy air | | | | | | | | | | |
| | | | | | | | | Operational assumptions for incremental analyses | | | | | | | | | | | | |
Tail type	Seats per tail	Number of tails in fleet	Total seats available per day	Length of operating day (in hours)	Weighted average duration of legs (in % of hour)	Average turn time	Total duration per leg (in % of hour)	Flights that could be flown in an operating day	Desired number of flights per operating day	Number of days in estimation period	Estimated load factor	Total theoretical hours	Estimated gate-to-gate hours	Estimated taxi & other airborne non-prod. (12.5 Minutes per flight)	Estimated load factor loss in hours	Estimated productive	Maintenance hours (0.37 Hrs per flight flown)	Total turn time	Estimated nonproductive hours	Estimated idle hours
200's	122	26	3,172	19	1.80	20	2.13	7	7	365	55.7%	227,760	119,676	13,840	46,845	58,991	2,458	22,143	85,286	22,798
300's	122	193	23,546	19	1.80	20	2.13	7	7	365	70.5%	1,690,680	888,364	102,732	231,826	553,806	18,245	164,372	517,175	285,141
500's	137	25	3,425	19	1.80	30	2.30	6	6	365	58.4%	219,000	98,634	11,406	36,292	50,936	2,026	27,375	77,099	43,267
700's	137	134	18,358	19	1.80	30	2.30	6	6	365	65.7%	1,173,840	528,679	61,138	160,397	307,144	10,858	146,730	379,123	266,038
Totals		378	48,501									3,311,280	1,635,353	189,116	475,360	970,877	33,587	360,620	1,058,683	617,244

Figure 11.2. Easy Air incremental analysis template.

how much it would cost if a change in the vacuum forming department was made. Once again, gathering the information to support the VCMS project resulted in information that could be used in a variety of ways internally to improve the quality and consistency of the incremental capacity utilization analysis done in the company. The results of a part of this analysis are demonstrated in Figure 11.3.

So what is the total information required to support the VCMS? First, if the company is a service company, the data includes the following:

	Category	Dollars 1999	% of total $'s	Dollars 1998	% of total $'s
Idle capacity	Management policy (holidays)	$86,666	0.4%	$86,970	0.4%
	Idle but usable	$1,013,087	4.2%	$1,109,167	5.2%
Total idle capacity		**$1,099,754**	**4.5%**	**$1,196,137**	**5.6%**
Nonproductive Capacity	Manned idle (unaccounted)	$3,235,291	13.3%	$1,202,148	5.6%
	Internal failure - cost of quality	$174,911	0.7%	$148,391	0.7%
	Material problems	$404,859	1.7%	$222,474	1.0%
	Machine breakdowns	$668,227	2.8%	$666,907	3.1%
	Scheduled	$-	0.0%	$-	0.0%
	Change-overs	$1,399,433	5.8%	$1,330,057	6.2%
	Clean-up	$135,513	0.6%	$116,700	0.5%
	Mgt. Policy (lunch, allowance)	$643,297	2.7%	$264,328	1.2%
	Material handling	$607,526	2.5%	$525,647	2.5%
	Mgt. Downtime (misc)	$687,812	2.8%	$1,699,373	8.0%
	Nonitemized downtime	$99,713	0.4%	$238,164	1.1%
Total nonproductive		**$8,056,583**	**33.2%**	**$6,414,190**	**30.0%**
Productive capacity	Manufacturing	$15,092,863	62.2%	$13,758,957	64.4%
	Developmental	$-	0.0%	$-	0.0%
Total productive		**$15,092,863**	**62.2%**	**$13,758,957**	**64.4%**
		$-	0.0%	$-	0.0%
Total capacity costs		**$24,249,200**	**100.0%**	**$21,369,284**	**100.0%**

Figure 11.3. Windows, Inc. capacity analysis.

- Activity analysis
- Customer profile data
- Mapping of activities to value-add, BVA-Indirect, BVA-Future, BVA-Administrative, and Waste categories
- Mapping of activities to value attributes.

If the company has manufacturing as part of its basic operations, capacity analysis needs to be added to the cost analysis segment to ensure that the data internal to the firm matches the activity analysis in a comprehensive way. In capacity analysis, the value-add portion of the capacity utilization is clearly outlined, with various forms of BVA-Administrative and waste activities clearly outlined. Since it takes more resources to collect the capacity data, even though it is minimized in nature, this is why VCMS works so well in service firms—the data collection is greatly minimized.

Whether in manufacturing or service, the VCMS supports consistent incremental analysis where the data is based on actual operations, not assumed relationships. This is a marked improvement over most existing incremental analysis where cost analysts assume new conditions for every decision. The VCMS results in a total costing approach that is driven by customer concerns first and foremost, but which can also be used to identify and isolate internal operational improvements with no, or minimal, new data collection needed.

Collecting and Using Data for Performance Evaluation

Supporting decision analysis, whether strategic or incremental in nature, is a natural outgrowth of using the VCMS approach to measure and manage a firm's cost and value structure. The question that immediately gets raised in most companies, though, is how to use the information to evaluate performance. The Windows, Inc. analysis noted above was done for all of the cost centers in the organization. This approach allowed management to compare the performance of the various cost centers to see where capacity utilization was high and where it needed to be addressed. The greater the amount of productive time on a machine, given what it produces is actually needed by the firm to meet customer demand, the greater the value-add component. Windows, Inc. relied heavily upon profit sharing with its employees to manage its workforce commitment to superior performance. The results of this type of reward's ability to motivate employees were seen in the very high utilizations of machinery across the company. No one was motivated to buy excess machinery.

Impact Communications also built the VCMS data into its performance evaluation process. Engagement managers were evaluated based on how closely they held the expenditures and efforts on a project to the value profile the customer had defined. This was a major change to the performance evaluation process, one that focused everyone's attention on the need to tailor each engagement so that individual customers would be satisfied with the outcomes. Since the firm needed to build up a loyal customer base, building the VCMS logic into performance evaluation helped ensure that satisfied customers would come back to the firm in the future.

There are many ways, then, that the VCMS data can be built into performance management systems. Cost centers can be held accountable for maximizing the value add component of their work and using continuous improvement methods to drive out waste and minimize BVA-administrative activities. Goals can be set for these cost reductions. If the resulting savings are reinvested into activities and outcomes that the customer base values, the firm can grow its value profile in ways that increase its competitiveness.

Elements of the VCMS puzzle can also be built into the performance evaluation system, as was seen at Windows, Inc. In this situation, the benefits gained can once again be used to create new funds for value-creating work. Identifying waste and eliminating it is always a good management approach. Knowing what to do with the funds that are freed up is a benefit of using the VCMS framework to manage the business.

One warning needs to be voiced at this stage, though. When the VCMS is used as a management control tool it becomes open to the same level of dysfunctional consequences as are seen in any control situation. While it is difficult to game the capacity analysis, it is possible that a cost center would overproduce to make its capacity utilization numbers look good. But, if the overproduction results in increased inventories and downstream damage or obsolescence of parts, it is not a win for the company. That means the information provided by the VCMS must be balanced off against other performance goals for the company or cost center.

Given its reliance on manager input to develop the activity analysis, using the VCMS for performance evaluation can also lead to managers claiming higher percentages of value-add activities even if their performance has not really changed. Since there are very few ways to verify this information, short of closely monitoring daily activities in a department, little is gained if the system leads to data manipulation or false reporting by cost center managers.

As with all information systems, then, the VCMS walks a fine line between positive and negative impacts when it is used for management control purposes. It is a reality faced in all organizations that people hate being controlled and will do many undesirable things to meet their goals if they feel pressure to meet preset standards. Using VCMS data for control purposes, then, must be done carefully or the integrity of the whole system can be impaired.

So, the question that results is: Should the VCMS be used for management control purposes at all? The answer is that clearly the information needs to be used at a high level to guide decisions that make the firm better at creating value for its customers. Pushing the control element lower in the organization, though, can lead to faulty information or other dysfunctional results that may damage the reliability of the information. It is the researchers' view, then, that using the VCMS for internal management control purposes should be done with great care or not at all. It is a decision support tool, not a management control one. There are many ways that performance can be monitored. If, for instance, managers feel that there is a reward for continuous improvement, this can result in distortions in the VCMS-reported results.

Taking a Temperature or Ongoing Monitoring?

A second question that often arises when the VCMS study is completed is whether or not the effort should be a one-time event or whether the reporting of VCMS data should become part of the regular monthly reporting package for cost centers. The answer to this question lies in what benefits the organization wishes to obtain from the VCMS. If it is done just to test the validity of the current strategy, it clearly can be done as a one-time study.

The results of a one-time study will be time sensitive, though, so the VCMS loses a lot of its ability to guide future actions. Since it becomes simpler for managers to provide the needed data the more often they actually perform the needed data collection and calculations, it makes some sense to build the VCMS into the monthly or quarterly reporting package for the firm. This is especially true if the data is to be used for incremental analysis. This is short-term decision-making, which means that data needs to be up-to-date and reliable.

If the firm only wishes to use the VCMS data for strategic planning, the data can probably be collected on an annual basis. In this case the focus would be on how much improvement there has been in meeting customer expectations. The study would also provide management with insights into whether customer preferences have changed over the past year. The combination of the two streams of VCMS-based data supports a fine-tuning of the firm's strategy to keep it constantly focused on meeting new and existing customer demands. If done yearly, the study should be handled by the internal control group of the organization as they are usually the most trusted and trained in the art of doing an information-gathering interview.

Regardless of whether the data is used solely for strategic analysis, or also put to use in incremental analysis, decisions need to be made about whose responsibility it should become to maintain the data files and resulting database. While the initial team might seem the best group to tap for this, the managers on the team will clearly have other tasks that they are expected to perform. It can be very difficult to maintain the initial implementation team as the organization goes through natural changes. This is why it is recommended that once the initial study is completed, the responsibility for maintaining the VCMS database fall to a group, such as the lean management or internal control organization, to ensure that it remains a top priority.

So the answer to the question about whether the VCMS should be a one-time study or become part of the ongoing reporting requirements in the organization is "it depends." It takes a significant amount of work to complete the initial data collection. Managers across the organization need to be trained in how to answer the questions and fill in the data forms. Capacity analysis needs to be undertaken if the organization has a manufacturing component. This is a lot of work to do to only use the results one time. Since it gets simpler to maintain the database the more frequently cost centers report on their activities, it seems logical to maintain the database with monthly or quarterly data collection so the greatest value can be obtained from the data embedded in the VCMS.

Making Value-Add a Mindset

If the VCMS becomes part of the regular reporting requirements of an organization, it helps to make value-add a mindset as part of the internal culture. Since meeting customer expectations on an ongoing basis is the key to gaining loyal customers, it is very important for the firm to do some form of value monitoring on an ongoing basis. Marketing clearly needs to be constantly polling the customer base to determine what their preferences are. If the industry is highly cost-competitive, there will be more and more of the organization's product or service features that will be folded into competitive price (table stakes). Competition constantly eats away at the benefits of a differentiation strategy. Only by staying on top of customer preferences can a firm stay ahead of the competition.

It is also important to make value-add a mindset because it helps guide internal decision-making. Instead of pushing for new equipment or personnel to gain personal power, the guiding question becomes "will this new expenditure improve our firm's value profile." A new logic, then, is created for making investments in the firm when value-add becomes part of the organizational mindset.

Ongoing use of the VCMS supports the embedding of a value-add mindset in an organization. By constantly drawing the conversation back to whether or not an activity or asset will improve the organization's ability to meet customer expectations, the VCMS makes value-add a visible part of the organization's daily functioning. Just as adding quality monitoring to the plant floor has served to improve quality in adopting organizations, the VCMS approach can improve the firm's ability to meet or exceed customer expectations. It supports the creation of a customer-centered organization.

Summary

In this chapter we've seen how the VCMS can be used in both strategic and incremental analysis. The information collected as part of the VCMS study is very useful in a variety of contexts. By tying everything constantly back to customer value-add the VCMS makes the concept of customer value visible and actionable within the organization. Ongoing maintenance of the VCMS database increases the reliability of the data, especially if it is used as a decision support tool rather than a management control tool.

In making value-add visible and actionable, the VCMS helps the organization stay focused on those value attributes preferred by its customers. Serving as a disciplining device, the VCMS makes it easier to make decisions about where investments should take place and where costs should be trimmed or controlled. While these benefits can come from a one-time study, the VCMS gains more power in the organizational culture if it becomes part of the ongoing reporting package.

Marketing or marketing intelligence clearly should be tasked with keeping their finger on the pulse of the customers and of the marketplace. By transforming the collected information into VCMS-friendly formats, the customer value expectations can be used to drive internal operations. An ongoing group, such as the lean management or internal control organization, should be placed in charge of the upkeep of the VCMS database. Whether updated monthly or quarterly, the VCMS has its greatest power if it is maintained. For companies that have manufacturing activities, monthly reporting makes the most sense. If the firm is purely service-oriented, quarterly reporting may suffice. The more frequently the data is collected, the greater its value as an information system.

Regardless of the use made of the VCMS data, it provides new insights and helps a company build a customer value-add mindset that can help differentiate it from its competitors. Strategic by design, and operational in nature, the VCMS is a valuable new form of reporting and decision support that can help transform a company into a value leader in its industry. It is a tool with many uses, creating a reliable, repeatable, and verifiable storehouse of decision support data.

Economy is half the battle of life; it is not so hard to earn money as to spend it well.

Spurgeon[3]

CHAPTER 12

Revisiting the Basics

It is good to have an end to journey toward;
but it is the journey that matters, in the end.
Ursula K. Le Guin[1]

The journey through the different aspects of the value-based cost management system (VCMS) is now complete. We've seen examples of many companies that have used the model in a variety of ways to address strategic, tactical, and operational problems. Some companies have built an entirely new control approach using the logic of customer value as the driving force. We've also seen how the VCMS fits seamlessly with many of the advanced management techniques, such as process management, value engineering, and target costing. It is a tool that starts from a set of simple assumptions and results in a rich body of knowledge about what a company does right—and wrong.

In this chapter we're going to summarize the basics of what has been presented in the previous pages. We will provide an overview of the model and how it has been used in participating organizations. The goal is to capture the knowledge and learning resulting from the VCMS. Let's start by reviewing the basics once more.

The VCMS Model—The Basics Revisited

The heart of the VCMS is its view of customer value in the marketplace and the internal cost structure of the firm. A second key element is the application of value attributes to the revenue stream to generate revenue equivalents. These two basic additions to the existing activity analysis literature result in a rich model that supports a wide range of decisions and actions. What did the basic cost breakdown of a firm look like from a market perspective? Figure 12.1 reintroduces the basic model.

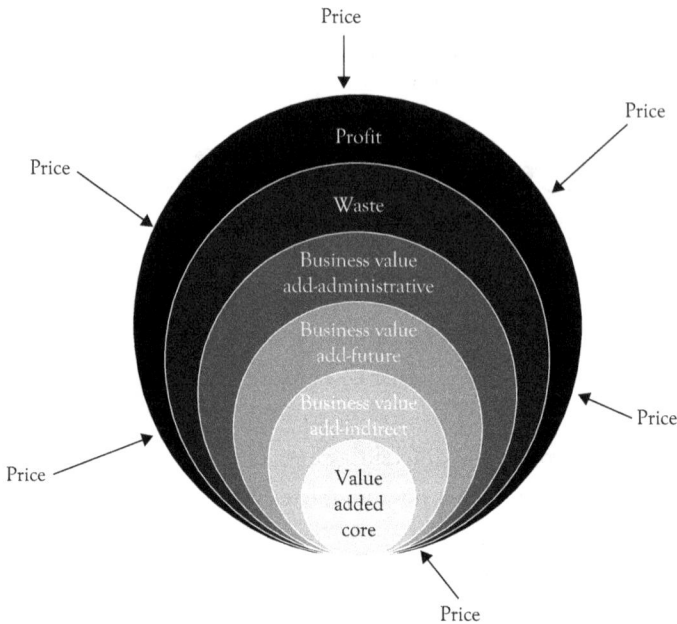

Figure 12.1. Cost from a market perspective.

The model begins by taking the market price as the disciplining factor in any company. Unless a firm operates in a pure monopoly, it doesn't control its final price. Most firms have some power over price but this power depends on the degree of competition in their markets. Successful companies have to master how to make a profit within the competitive constraints of their markets. The competitive marketplace is constantly putting pressure on this price window, as company after company seeks to gain business by offering the same or slightly different products and services for less money. Price, then, sets an outside limit on how much a profit-making organization can afford to spend to deliver a specific product or service.

The spending that generates the price of a product is called the value-added core of activities. In our field work we found value-added core to represent about 20–25% of the total spending in a company. The value-added core is to be protected at all costs. This is one of the key lessons learned—spending cuts should never target those activities qualified as customer value-add. To cut the value-added core results in a collapse of the value profile of the firm, reducing the price a customer might be willing to pay for the affected product or service. The value-added core is supported by many individuals in the organization, either directly or indirectly. No one activity is purely value-add or nonvalue-add because activities consist of tasks, some more valuable to the customer than others.

The value-added core consists of a set of value attributes that combine to make the value profile of a product or service. The VCMS uses this value profile to develop revenue equivalents, or estimates of how much of the revenue earned is based on specific value attributes. The information for the weighting of the value attributes in the value profile is developed using customer data. In our work we often found that management did not truly understand the value profile of its customers and how much different value attributes are worth in the overall profile.

Combining the revenue equivalents with the value-added costs provides a series of value multipliers. These multipliers are strategic signals about how effectively the firm is using its resources and thereby spending its money. If a value multiplier is low (below four), it means the firm is spending too much to deliver on that value attribute. If the multiplier is high (greater than seven), it can either be a competitive advantage—the firm is really good at delivering this component of value—or the company is under-spending on the attribute, resulting in dissatisfied customers. In this manner the VCMS provides detailed signals to management about how effectively they are using the organization's funds to create the right type of value for their customers.

Beyond Value-Add

The first ring out from value-add in Figure 12.1 is the Business Value-Add—indirect (BVA_i). This consists of all of the aspects of an activity that could result in an unhappy customer if not done well. Some companies, such as Easy Air, have decided that these activities are so important to the overall experience a customer has with a company that they should be included in the value-based analysis of the firm. Most other companies have left them out of value-add because they really do not generate price, they only affect satisfaction. Since a satisfied customer is more likely to become a loyal customer, though, there is ample evidence to say that these activities and their underlying tasks need to be carefully studied to ensure they are done well. Cost cutting in this category should be done with care, with a constant eye toward the ultimate impact on the customer's experience with the organization.

Next we see Business Value-Add—future (BVA_F). The activities in this ring are all of the things a company does to ensure that it has something to offer to future customers. Consisting of things such as research and development and marketing efforts, these activities are critical from the perspective of the firm's owners. Only firms that continue to innovate can truly compete in the long run in the marketplace. The dollars spent in this category are an investment of funds from today's sales that helps ensure that the organization remains viable in the future. These are not discretionary expenditures, as financial accounting tags them, but vital for the health of the organization. Cost cutting should not take place here unless there are no other options left to the firm.

The third ring out from the value-added core is Business Value-Add—administrative (BVA_A). Here we see all of the activities and tasks that are undertaken solely to support the functioning of the organization—they don't result in any revenue today or tomorrow. A customer doesn't care how a company manages itself. Since there is no value-add in these activities, they should be carefully monitored to ensure they don't grow beyond a reasonable level. In our work we found this level to be at about 10–15% of the total revenues earned. As companies mature, we often notice that BVA_A activities begin to consume more and more of the scarce dollars earned by the value-added core of the product and service attributes. When cost cutting needs to take place, this is one of the first places the firm should review. It is no accident that the majority of the lean management exercises emphasize administrative tasks—they simply add no value to the customer.

Waste is the fourth ring out. There is no benefit to either the organization or the customer from waste. Whether it comes from rework, excess processing, or even excess value in a product, it is to be eliminated wherever it occurs. One of the simplest examples of how a company can actually create waste with something that probably was considered by management to be part of the value-added core is Tupperware*. This is a product that is built to last, but unfortunately the original owner seldom gets to use up the value in the product—the pieces end up in someone else's kitchen (most likely one's children), being used but not by the person who paid the premium price for the product. This excess value led to the creation of more disposable, and much less expensive, market alternatives to the Tupperware® brand. The excess value ends up being waste to the consumer who purchased the product. Clearly this isn't the case for all of the products made by this company, but it does apply to many of their offerings.

Finally, given the market conditions, and if resources were consumed with care by the activities of the firm, the company might generate positive profit. There is always a squeeze on profit, though, as market forces continue to put pressure on price, one of the boundaries of profit, and internal costs tend to creep over time, putting pressure on profit's other boundary. Protecting the company profit starts by understanding how resources are consumed and using disciplined approaches to minimize internal cost increases.

The VCMS model, then, allows a firm to separate out the various types of costs at the activity level, implicitly tying the costing process to the tasks that make up an activity. While an activity may be 30% value-add, there is undoubtedly some BVA_A required to meet internal communication needs. And, some level of waste exists in most activities that are performed in a company. Getting rid of this waste has spawned an entire discipline—lean management. The VCMS supports lean management by identifying those activities where waste is hidden, helping to prioritize improvement efforts.

Strategic, Tactical, and Operational Uses of the VCMS

The value multipliers developed as part of a VCMS study are one of the ways in which the model provides strategic information to a firm. As we saw at both GTI and Impact Communications, this information can serve as a surprise—management learns they are not putting the firm's resources into the right activities. We also learned that customers can often be segmented by offering different products that have different value profiles. This can be a challenge for a firm that is used to providing the same product to all its customers. Different customer segments require different types of effort from the firm.

As we saw at Windows, Inc. their grouping of value profiles led to the definition of separate segments consisting of architects and small builders. These segments have important power in the value chain but they are not the final customers of the product. They may influence the buying decision, and they most likely insert additional demands on the company's resources in the buying process. Managing these business-to-business activities has to be done with an eye on the additional costs and benefits incurred, given that they are most often BVA$_A$ activities in the customer's eyes. Since these activities can reduce profit, they have to be performed as efficiently as possible. In our field work with Windows, Inc. we found that these trading partners were important for them and that it was in their best interest to understand their needs and see how best to meet them in order to protect profitability and value delivered to final customers. That being said, these costs still had to be managed with an eye toward protecting profitability.

The VCMS was originally designed as a strategic tool, but once it was implemented in companies it began to be apparent that the depth of the activity analysis additionally supported both tactical and operational decision-making. At the tactical level, the VCMS supports three key modern management models—value engineering, target costing, and lean management. For target costing and value engineering, the customer data can be immediately matched up with the internal activities required to deliver specific customer value. This is most valuable in the support dimension, where the traditional flat overhead rate is replaced by activity-specific costs. At Windows, Inc. a series of product development decisions was supported by the VCMS model. This included the tactical decision about many different sizes and colors of windows and doors were needed to gain a foothold in the marketplace with their new product line.

Easy Air used the VCMS data in a tactical way to study their routing structure and change these structures as a result of information provided by the VCMS. For instance, the VCMS data helped support incremental analysis of the differences between short-haul and long-haul flights. The result was to create a separate customer segment for the long-haul planes. By changing the way the management thought about long-haul flights, decoupling them from regional systems, the firm was able to improve its on-time performance rating, one of the critical statistics measuring airline quality. Since long-haul planes dragged variation with them from one coast to another, this decoupling allowed the company to neutralize this excess variation and return to better performance overall.

Impact Communications also made a combination of strategic, tactical, and operational changes to their operations based on the VCMS-based learning. Discovering that they were only serving one segment of their customer population well, two major changes were made. Structurally, resources were shifted from the research activity to the publicity activities in the firm. This was a major cultural change, as the firm had grown up around the research skills of its founder.

A second operational change was then made at Impact Communications. Engagement discussions with customers were altered to include a discussion of how the customer wanted the firm to spend their engagement dollars—what value attributes were most important to the customer. This new information was used to guide the development of the engagement plan and to report back to customers as the job progressed. These changes helped to create a new focus for the company's employees, one that was more aligned with their strategic markets and their needs.

Tying VCMS to Other Initiatives

As has been noted throughout this discussion, the VCMS is a natural partner to several other modern management techniques used in organizations today. First and foremost, it supports process management. The process codes for activities can be built directly into the data collection effort. Using a framework, such as the APQC model, we have seen how the process information can be developed.

At the USCGA, process coding allowed the organization to understand how much value it was delivering and where. The organization had never taken a process view of its operations before, so the new insights were quite valuable. While most of the resources were directed toward cadets in today's program, significant resources were directed toward the processes needed to identify and obtain new cadets that met the rigorous acceptance criteria for the USCGA. The organization also spent significant funds maintaining its physical and financial resources—these were the highest processes in terms of total cost and time. Tied to the structure of the organization, it was difficult for the USCGA to change its process spending, but putting new light on this spending led to discussions to renegotiate some of the contracts used for outsourcing some of the maintenance work on campus.

Easy Air also performed extensive process coding during the collection phase. Since the firm was so committed to customer service, they were pleasantly surprised when the combination of direct and indirect value-add was so high for the processes that mattered to customers. This didn't lead to change, as the firm was satisfied that it was directing it operational funds in the right places. It reinforced that management had a good handle on how best to serve the customer.

We have also noted that the VCMS supports target costing. At Windows, Inc. the cost breakdown for the new window was estimated using proxies from the data collection phase of the VCMS. Using the existing structure of the organization, costs were assigned across the five categories of value-add itself, BVA_I, BVA_P, BVA_A, and waste. This knowledge triggered an intense focus on disciplining the spending on nonvalue-adding activities, leading to a change in how supplier relationships were handled, including the use of the firm's own vacuum forming operation. Unnecessary paperwork was eliminated as a streamlined back office set of routines was developed. The new window was not launched immediately because it couldn't meet its target cost, but additional value engineering finally led to the successful release of the new product line several years later.

The VCMS supports value engineering by matching up the value attributes with the current costs to deliver on those attributes. What is added to value engineering is the further breakdown of the support costs into specific activities, which can then become the target for reduction as was seen at Windows, Inc. At Frangor, the information from the study led the value engineering team to decide to move to platforms, or families, of products rather than the one-up approach that had been used in the past. This helped reduce raw materials inventories significantly, helping the company to improve its profit picture.

Lean management and the VCMS are natural partners in any organization. Since the VCMS identifies the waste and BVA_A levels in the various activities, it supports the prioritization of lean management projects. Since lean management targets the elimination of waste through continuous improvement and process redesign, the information provided by the VCMS can support these efforts, providing information both before and after the process redesign on whether costs have been trimmed. The VCMS was indirectly used by the U.S. Coast Guard Financial Center when it implemented lean management. The categorization of costs by the redesign team allowed the team to focus the new process design to augment the value-adding activities and reduce or eliminate much of the paperwork that had been clogging the system. The result was that the organization was able to take many more of the available prompt payment discounts, saving a significant amount of money in the first few months following the redesign effort. This was money that could be redirected to putting fuel in ships so that they could do more missions—a value-add improvement for the nation.

The VCMS is a natural part of strategic cost analysis, as was once again seen at Frangor. While Frangor gained insights from using the traditional strategic cost categorization of structural and executional cost drivers, it wasn't until the VCMS study was done that truly actionable information was gained. The VCMS is an extension of strategic cost analysis, one that puts customer-defined value attributes in the driver's seat for making strategic changes. If savings are reinvested in the value-adding core, the result is a model of growth that helps an organization to accomplish its profitability goals.

Implementation of the VCMS

The implementation of the VCMS starts with customer value data and a clear understanding of the importance of the different value attributes used in customer decisions. Data collection is often done in marketing research departments or data can be purchased from outside vendors. Customer value data is then transformed to the 100 point system necessary for the VCMS using a variety of methods. It is important for the VCMS and its implementation to use current customer data and for the data to reflect a solid understanding of critical attributes and their importance for customer decision-making in relevant markets. When time is of the essence and resources are limited, customer focus groups can be used to obtain customer value information. At Easy Air, surveys were sent to the firm's frequent flyers to gather this information. Regardless of the method used to collect customer data and value attribute information, it is the starting point for the implementation of the VCMS.

Once the value attributes have been identified, attention turns to gathering internal activity analysis data, which is augmented by process coding in some instances. If process coding isn't used, then the data collection effort focuses down on classifying the costs spent on an activity to one of the five subcategories of cost. Value-add costs are then assigned to specific value attributes. This data collection effort is supported by software such as an integrated Excel spreadsheet that both tallies the key data points for the respondent and, with the simple addition of a budget figure, results in cost by attribute and category. These data can be combined into either one master data file or a relational database. The relational approach offers more flexibility in the analysis phase and is recommended.

Once all of the data has been collected, a number of reports can be generated, such as a report on where primary value-add is taking place. The data also supports the development of value multipliers, which detail how well the firm is meeting customer value preferences. Very low multipliers mean the firm is overspending on delivering a value attribute. This is the case if the multiplier is below 4. Five is a target number as most firms have been found to have roughly 20% value-added costs in their structure. High multipliers are more difficult to interpret. If the customer is very satisfied with the firm's performance on an attribute with a high multiplier, then the firm has a competitive advantage. If customers are dissatisfied, however, the firm has a strategic weakness that must be addressed by focusing more resources on the underserved attribute.

During implementation, decisions have to be made as to whether the VCMS study is a one-time event or a new part of the ongoing reporting package of the firm. In most of the companies studied, it was a one-time event. The exception was Impact Communication, where the data was used to create a new management control system that ensured that client engagement dollars were spent according to customer preferences. Building the VCMS into the ongoing reporting package optimizes the impact of this new information and perspective on the adopting organization. If properly administered, it becomes relatively inexpensive to maintain the data on a monthly, quarterly, or annual basis. This is the recommended approach.

Finally, there is always a question about whether a new tool should be coupled with the firm's management control system. This is not always a good idea as it can lead to false reporting as managers might seek to prove they are value-adding in their activities. Since the data collection process is dependent on accurate reporting by managers, it is important to remember that management control uses of data is a double-edged sword. More control is clearly gained, as attention is shifted to the value attributes, as seen at Impact Communications. But, managers might be less likely to report accurately if they are given targeted levels of value-add. The only way changes can occur in the value component of work is if it is redesigned to optimize the value-adding components. Simply putting a goal out there without providing the tools to reach those goals is counterproductive. Building the VCMS into the firm's control system, then, should be done with great care. Making value add visible is one thing, holding managers accountable for value-add components when they can't really control those components can lead to suboptimal behavior and incentive conflicts.

Summary

The VCMS provides a new language for the firm, one that unites everyone around customer value and market perspective of the firm. At Windows, Inc. one of the major benefits gained from its VCMS implementation was that marketing and finance could now communicate more clearly about key goals and results in the firm. The VCMS, then, is a way to bridge the gap between different functional areas in the organization, tying everyone to the customer.

The VCMS model works very well in service organizations. In manufacturing organizations, a further implementation of capacity cost management is useful. This is valuable information for the firm, and has been found to be sustained by the firms as an ongoing reporting package. The breakdown of capacity information into value-add and nonvalue-add components is relatively straightforward.[2] This technique was used in many of the firms studied during the VCMS project—it is a critical tool for proper implementation in any setting where machine-paced work exists.

In the end, a company implementing VCMS can decide to use the information for a broad range of strategic, tactical, and operational decisions. Because the VCMS integrates with many of today's advanced management techniques, it can serve multiple uses in multiple settings. Creating a new language, one that focuses everyone's eyes on the customer and customer value, it helps create the customer-centered organization. When finance embraces the customer in its reporting packages, the entire organization wins. It is a journey with many benefits, one that begins with understanding customer preferences and ends with making sure they are used to drive internal operations and decision-making.

> *To be what we are, and to become what we are capable of becoming is the only end of life.*
>
> Spinoza[3]

Notes

Chapter 1

1. McKenzie (1980), p. 533.
2. This definition is based on that presented in a short essay by Geraerdts (2012), p. 11.
3. Preim (2007), p. 219.
4. Preim (2007), p. 220.
5. Gronroos (2011).
6. Blattberg, Getz, and Thomas (2001), p. 10.

Chapter 2

1. Ronnback et al. (2009), p. 241.
2. Nagle and Holden (1999).
3. This example was originally published in *The Profit Potential: Taking High Performance to the Bottom Line* by C. J. McNair (Connolly) in 1994, p. 51. The company involved has since used the information contained in this example to radically transform their service function. While the firm must remain anonymous in this work, let it suffice to say that the company is a household word in today's electronically-driven world.
4. Dividing the 60% of excess cost spent on manuals by the 70% of the total amount of the department's budget spent on manuals results in an estimate of 89% waste, or excess spending on manual production and maintenance.
5. Smith and Nagle (1994), pp. 71–84.
6. Impact Communications is a pseudonym that was developed during work with this specific client.
7. Bolander (1991).

Chapter 3

1. Klein (2005), p. 130.
2. Gronroos (2011).
3. Klein (2005), p. 233.

Chapter 4

1. Ford (1926), p. 93.
2. McNair (1994), p. 5.
3. Keyte and Locher (2004), pp. 1–2.
4. This discussion is based on information and data first published by McNair (1994), pp. 24–34.
5. McNair (1994), p. 230.
6. Peter (1979).

Chapter 5

1. Peter (1979).
2. The data underlying this table was originally published in McNair et al. (2001), p. 42.
3. This discussion is based on data collected during the development of the case Impact Communications for Babson College's case series. The data is transformed uniquely for this book using tables that appeared in the case teaching notes.
4. In reality, revenue/value multipliers exist on a continuum ranging from zero to infinity. While we have found these multipliers to range anywhere from 0.5 to 50, the fact that only a few companies have been visited suggests that even a greater range of multipliers likely exists.
5. Galbraith (2005), p. 9.

Chapter 6

1. Klein (2005), p. 277.
2. Green and Srinivasan (1990).
3. Klein (2005), p. 19.

Chapter 7

1. Klein (2005), p. 112.
2. Klein (2005), p. 131.

Chapter 8

1. Forbes (1992), p. 112.
2. This section makes heavy use of the white paper by Brache (2012) found on the company website.

3. Brache (2012), p. 4.
4. APQC International (1992), p. 2.
5. Klein (2005), p. 191.

Chapter 9

1. Klein (2005), p. 19.
2. Klein (2005), p. 129.

Chapter 10

1. The *Forbes Scrapbook* (1992), p. 1.
2. Berliner and Brimson (1988).
3. This organization, namely the Consortium for Advanced Manufacturing, International, has served as a thought leader in the field of Cost Management for over 25 years. It is headquartered in Dallas, TX and includes a broad range of manufacturing, service, and public organizations seeking to improve organizational performance through the application of advanced management tools.
4. The *Forbes Scrapbook* (1992), p. 48.

Chapter 11

1. The *Forbes Scrapbook* (1992), p. 178.
2. McNair and Vangermeersch (1999).
3. The *Forbes Scrapbook* (1992), p. 362.

Chapter 12

1. Klein (2005), p. 246.
2. For more information on this approach to manufacturing management, the reader is encouraged to review *Total Capacity Management* by McNair, C.J. and R. Vangermeersch (1998).
3. The *Forbes Scrapbook* (1992), p. 112.

References

APQC International Benchmarking Clearinghouse. (1992). *Process classification framework*. Houston: APQC International.

Berliner, C., & Brimson, J. (1988). *Cost management for today's advanced manufacturing*. Boston: Harvard Business School Press.

Blattberg, R. C., Getz, G., & Thomas, J. S. (2001). *Customer equity: Building and managing relationships as valuable assets*. Boston, MA: Harvard Business School Press.

Bolander, D. O. (Ed.), (1991). *The new webster's dictionary of quotes and famous phrases*. New York, NY: Berkley Books.

Brache, A. (2012). *What is a process? why should you care?* Retrieved December 1, 2012, From www.rummler-brache.com/case-studies-and-white-papers.

Forbes. (1992). *The forbes scrapbook of thoughts on the business of life*. Chicago: Triumph Books.

Ford, H. (1926). *Today and tomorrow*. New York: Doubleday, Page.

Galbraith, J. (2005). *Designing the customer-centric organization*. San Francisco: Jossey-Bass.

Geraerdts, R. (2012). Customer value creation: A journey in the search of excellence. *Industrial Marketing Management 41*, 11–12.

Green, P. E., & Srinivasan, V. (1990). Conjoint analysis in marketing: new development with implications for research and practice. *Journal of Marketing 54*, 3–19.

Gronroos, C. (2011). A service perspective on business relationships: The value creation, interaction, and marketing interface. *Industrial Marketing Management 40*, 240–247.

Keyte, B., & Locher, D. (2004). *The complete lean enterprise: Value stream mapping for administrative and office processes*. New York: Productivity Press.

Klein, A. (2005). *The wise and witty quote book*. New York: Gramercy Books.

McKenzie, E. (1980). *14,000 quips & quotes*. New York: Wings Books.

McNair, C. (1994). *The profit potential: Taking high performance to the bottom line*. Essex Junction, VT: Omneo.

McNair, C., Polutnik, L., & Silvi, R. (2001). Outside-In: Cost and the creation of customer value. M. Epstein (Ed.) *Advances in Management Accounting 9*, 1–42.

McNair, C., Silvi, R., & Polutnik, L. (2001). Cost management and value creation: the missing link. *European Accounting Review 10*(1), 33–50.

McNair, C., & Vangermeersch, R. (1999). *Total capacity management: Optimizing at the operational, tactical and strategic levels.* Boca Raton, Fl: St. Lucie Press.

Nagle, T. T., & Holden, R. K. (1999). *Strategy and the tactics of pricing* (2nd Edn.). Englewood Cliffs, NJ: Prentice-Hall.

Peter, L. J. (1979). *Peter's quotations: Ideas for our times.* New York: Bantam Books.

Priem, R. (2007). A consumer perspective on value creation. *Academy of Management Review 22*(1), 219–235.

Ronnback, A., Witell, L., & Enquist, B. (2009). Quality management systems and value creation. *International Journal of Quality and Service Sciences 1*(3), 241–254.

Smith, G., & Nagle, T. (1994). Financial analysis for profit-driven pricing. *Sloan Management Review 35*(1), 71–84.

Index

OTHER TITLES IN THE MANAGERIAL ACCOUNTING COLLECTION

Kenneth A. Merchant, University of Southern California, Collection Editor

- *The Small Business Controller* by Richard O. Hanson
- *Sustainability Reporting: Managing for Wealth and Corporate Health* by Gwendolen B. White
- *Business Planning and Entrepreneurship: An Accounting Approach* by Michael Kraten
- *Corporate Investment Decisions: Principles and Practice* by Michael Pogue
- *Drivers of Successful Controllership: Activities, People, and Connecting with Management* by Jurgen Weber and Pascal Nevries
- *Revenue Management: A Path to Increased Profits* by Ronald Huefner
- *Cost Management and Control in Government: Fighting the Cost War Through Leadership Driven Management* by Dale Geiger
- *Setting Performance Targets* by Carolyn Stringer and Paul Shantapriyan
- *Strategic Cost Analysis* by Roger Hussey and Audra Ong
- *Customer-Driven Budgeting Prepare, Engage, Execute: The Small Business Guide for Growth* by Floyd Talbot
- *Economic Decision Making Using Cost Data: A Guide for Managers* by Daniel M. Marburger and Ryan Peterson
- *Breakeven Analysis: The Definitive Guide to Cost-Volume-Profit Analysis* by Michael Cafferky and Jon Wentworth
- *Revenue Management in Service Organizations* by Paul Rouse, William McGuire, and Julie Harrison

Announcing the Business Expert Press Digital Library

Concise E-books Business Students Need for Classroom and Research

This book can also be purchased in an e-book collection by your library as
- a one-time purchase,
- that is owned forever,
- allows for simultaneous readers,
- has no restrictions on printing, and
- can be downloaded as PDFs from within the library community.

Our digital library collections are a great solution to beat the rising cost of textbooks. e-books can be loaded into their course management systems or onto student's e-book readers.

The **Business Expert Press** digital libraries are very affordable, with no obligation to buy in future years. For more information, please visit **www.businessexpertpress.com/librarians**. To set up a trial in the United States, please contact **Adam Chesler** at *adam.chesler@ businessexpertpress.com* for all other regions, contact **Nicole Lee** at *nicole.lee@igroupnet.com*.

www.ingramcontent.com/pod-product-compliance
Lightning Source LLC
Chambersburg PA
CBHW060553210326
41519CB00014B/3457